Ballet
Life
Behind
the
Scenes

Also by the Author

On Your Toes

From Classes, Rehearsals, and Performances
to the Company and Home Lives of the Dancers

Ballet Life Behind the Scenes

by Wendy Neale
Photographs by Steven Caras

A Herbert Michelman Book
CROWN PUBLISHERS, INC.   NEW YORK

For Camilla

11623329

Grateful acknowledgment is made to the Institute of Choreology for permission to reproduce the Benesh Movement Notation excerpt which appears on page 65, Benesh Movement Notation © Rudolf Benesh, London, 1955, and *Voluntaries* choreography © Glen Tetley, Stuttgart, 1973.

Published by Crown Publishers, Inc., One Park Avenue, New York, New York 10016, and simultaneously in Canada by General Publishing Company Limited

Manufactured in the United States of America

Library of Congress Cataloging in Publication Data

Neale, Wendy.
Ballet life behind the scenes.

"A Herbert Michelman book."
Includes index.
1. Ballet. I. Title.
GV1787.N35 1982   792.8   82-2429
ISBN: 0-517-541742   AACR2

Design by Joanna Nelson

10 9 8 7 6 5 4 3 2 1

First Edition

Contents

Acknowledgments

I would like to thank all the people in this book who have given so freely and generously of their time. American Ballet Theatre and the New York City Ballet were always willing to assist with any request, sometimes at very short notice. I am especially grateful to all those artists and administrative personnel from both companies who allowed me freedom of access to classes and rehearsals, and to be backstage or in the wings during performances. In addition to all the artists quoted or mentioned in these pages I would like to acknowledge the assistance of the following people from American Ballet Theatre: Charles France, assistant to the artistic director; Joyce A. Moffatt, former general manager; Jerry Rice, former production stage manager; Florence Pettan, coordinator for the artistic staff; Robert Pontarelli, director of press and public relations; Ann Barlow, former rehearsal coordinator; Gary B. Dunning, assistant manager; Elena Gordon, press assistant; and Wendy Walker, choreologist (Benesh Notation). Miss Walker, who joined the company not long before choreologist Dora Frankel left, has been consistently helpful.

I truly appreciate the time taken by the following in granting me interviews: Clive Barnes, Dr. William Hamilton, Dr. Peter Bullough, Dr. E. J. Langner, Dr. Rose Smart, Dr. Hsu and interpreter David Fung, Dr. Albert Ellis, and Robert Legrand. The Dance Research Department at Lincoln Center Public Library for the Performing Arts proved as indispensable as always. For their assistance and moral support throughout this project, a bow to Nicholas Grimaldi of the National Association for Regional Ballet, Lynn Ramsey, Claire Khalil, and David Barg.

1

Beginnings

One morning in the early 1950s, a young girl left her home in Leningrad to pay a visit to the Leningrad Ballet School.* She was curious, for it was the school from which the illustrious Kirov Ballet recruited its dancers—the company through which many of the great artists made their names.

The girl had no thought of becoming a ballet dancer; nothing could have been further from her mind. Maybe the art had touched her romantic instincts, but for the moment it was her sense of adventure that drew her to the school.

She was a good student, exceptionally bright, and her parents looked forward to the day when their daughter would be accepted into one of the professions. Her future seemed obvious.

As she made her way to the Leningrad Ballet School, her mind was filled with what she knew of it and what she imagined it to be like. She knew that those who trained at the institution, totally devoted to their art, spent an almost monastic life. The only difference was that the intangible ideal was art rather than religion. She did not know what she would experience at the school, but hoped at least she might be allowed to see students in a ballet class. Without her knowing it, this was to be an experience that would change her life.

When she arrived at the school, events took an unexpected turn. Whether her potential was instantly sensed or this happened to all children who walked through the front door of the school did not matter—she was instantly led to the doctor's office. There she was weighed and given a thorough physical examination and her proportions were measured. The director of the school was telephoned and told there was a promising potential student he should see. He went

* Since renamed the Vaganova Ballet School, after Agrippina Vaganova, great Russian master of the dance.

1

to investigate and, after further discussion, approached the girl, took one of her legs in his hands, and raised it to the side to see how high it would go. He was very impressed by her extension and flexibility.

The girl was then asked for her telephone number, as the school wanted to call her parents to propose that she study at the Leningrad Ballet School. The girl, stunned, since she knew her parents would never approve, gave the first number that came into her head. She wanted to be sure that her parents did not receive a phone call. Feeling sure that she had saved herself, she left, expecting the experience to remain nothing more than a pleasant memory. The day would come when she would be able to tell her parents what might have happened. What she did not realize was that, although she had left behind the wrong phone number, she had also left behind her name, and that would turn out to be her glass slipper.

Once they had found the girl's parents, the authorities of the Leningrad Ballet School met with unexpected resistance. Pleased though the parents may have been that their daughter had aroused such interest, their minds were filled with the typical doubts that disturb many parents faced with the possibility of their child having a career in the arts. Would she complete her training? If that happened, how successful would be her career? Did she really have the potential the teachers at the school claimed for her? Perhaps most important of all, did she have the stamina and temperament needed to survive the rigorous years of unrelenting work and self-discipline? Her parents were not at all sure that the child's potentially bright academic future should be pushed aside.

Most of the students begin their studies at the age of nine, but the Leningrad Ballet School had decided to take a group of students aged thirteen to fourteen and put them into an experimental class. This young girl was then thirteen years of age.

Finally, she was allowed to enter the school, and thus began the career of Natalia Makarova.

Some children start preballet at the age of three or four with a burning ambition to be a ballerina or danseur noble—others begin thinking they already are. Many are sent by parents who hope their children will live out their own thwarted childhood ambitions through successful careers. Certain children start as part of a "well-rounded education," which will include tap dancing and learning to play the piano. The parents look for signs of a Mikhail Baryshnikov, Fred Astaire, or Artur Rubinstein, and some parents would frown on their children achieving anything less than the accomplishments of all three.

Of the countless children who start to take ballet, the majority lose interest within a few years, or even weeks. Among those who become professionals, very few enter the top three American companies—American Ballet Theatre, New York City Ballet, and the Joffrey Ballet—since their combined total is fewer than two hundred and fifty dancers. Many more will join regional companies, which each year undergo several weeks without work, if not longer.

Industriousness and determination are needed to enter a company and also to maintain a place within it. Most dancers do not go beyond the corps de ballet, and of those who become soloists, a very few later become principals. A small number become masters whose names will be remembered.

In recent years ballet has achieved widespread popularity, and now girls and boys are studying the art in ever-increasing numbers.

There was a time when the embarrassing shortage of boys in ballet class was matched only by a boy's embarrassment at being present. Now that ballet is being recognized for the superior athleticism required, as well as for its artistic qualities, the percentage of boys to girls is increasing. The finely toned, sculpturesquely beautiful bodies of male ballet dancers have made their impact. With so many more boys able to see ballet performances, they are increasingly inclined to model themselves on the male dancer, rather than on the macho heroes of the past.

As this development is so recent, many of today's most successful principal dancers did everything possible, when they were young, to prevent their peers from knowing they studied ballet. Many had to prove their strength in fights, for they were frequently challenged. Patrick Bissell, with American Ballet Theatre, was dragged into fights so many times that his teachers considered him a troublemaker and warned others to stay away from him. He was raised in a farming town in Ohio, where boys who studied ballet were virtually ostracized, and Patrick spent progressively more time at the studios. At school, his grades reflected his unhappiness. The situation became so bad that at one point Patrick stopped dancing altogether, but his time away from ballet was short-lived, and his enthusiasm and friends drew him back to class. After that, he tolerated school until he went to study at the North Carolina School of the Arts, the place he feels turned him from a student into a professional dancer.

During his days at the Royal Danish Ballet School, Peter Martins, of the New York City Ballet, would cross the street to avoid boys who shouted insults, but although they hurt him, he had more sympathy than animosity for such children. He considered them rather stupid, and hoped that one day they would learn to appreciate the value of ballet. During the early years he hung on because he made friends at the studios and because he was sufficiently interested. As time went by, he developed a sense of responsibility toward his studies, and from the age of sixteen his talent became increasingly recognized.

Anthony Dowell, whose home company is the Royal Ballet, would never name Sadler's Wells Ballet School* when asked where he studied. This occurred frequently, since each day the schoolchildren in the area would meet at the train station from which they traveled home. Those years were not easy, especially as Anthony joined the school when he was eight years old, and found dancing very boring. It was love of painting and his model theatre that helped him survive the early years.

The art of ballet, which requires total dedication from such an early age, ensures that only the fittest survive to the point of entering a company. As if in contradiction to this, companies are filled with dancers at all levels who first studied for the most unlikely reasons.

Forbidden fruit, loss of appetite, and a pancake house on Route 4 in New Jersey were the originators of three men's careers in ballet. Ivan Nagy developed an intense enthusiasm because his parents hoped he would be the only one of their three children who would follow interests other than ballet; Fernando Bujones was first sent to class at his home in Havana on the advice of a psychiatrist because he would not eat; and Steven Caras became acquainted with a girl student of the American Ballet Center (now the Joffrey Ballet School) because he had a sudden urge one day to eat pancakes. Their chance meeting resulted in Steven's being offered a scholarship to the school.

As he tasted the forbidden fruit, Ivan Nagy learned how bitter it could be. He joined Hungary's professional dance school in Budapest when he was six, one of forty-eight to be accepted out of five thousand applicants. He soon discovered that life at school, away from his parents at this tender age, was a very harsh experience. The school had to stop the Sunday visits from his parents because they were too disrupting. "Every week was the same. On Sundays they would come to see me, so on Mondays I was temporarily disconnected and crying hysterically. On Tuesdays I was miserable, and on Wednesdays I progressed to mere melancholy. On Thursdays, Fridays, and Saturdays things became progressively better as we got nearer to Sunday. Then the great day would arrive, and on Mondays I'd be hysterical again." For the first two weeks after his parents' visits were stopped, Ivan remained highly disturbed. Soon, however, he calmed down enough to see through his tears, and started to progress very rapidly. It was a difficult childhood, and in recent years Ivan Nagy has become more acutely aware of the frustrations that he felt as a young boy, forced to live in a strict

* It became the Royal Ballet School in 1956.

environment without the nearness of his parents—a high price to pay, even for one of the world's best ballet trainings.

Sallie Wilson, former American Ballet Theatre principal, had a somewhat more romantic, if no less coincidental, beginning than the three boys. She initially played the violin. One night, when she was playing in the school orchestra for a ballet performance, the lights went out in the orchestra pit, and the instrumentalists were forced to play from memory. This gave Sallie her first opportunity to watch the performance. She was so impressed she decided that she would rather be dancing on the stage than playing in the orchestra pit below it. Sallie then started the study of ballet, at the age of twelve.

As a young boy, Bart Cook, now a principal with the New York City Ballet, wanted to become a member of the local boy choir in Ogden, Utah. The reason for his interest was not a yearning to be a singer but the chance to travel east with the choir. By the time Bart was old enough to enter it, the choir had been disbanded, and as an alternative he studied tap, ballet, and singing—all with the same teacher. Instead of singing the great choral works, Bart would sing "Shuffle Off to Buffalo" and follow it with a tap dance. In those days, ballet was a sideline that he found quite agreeable, because he would occasionally perform in a recital. Since Bart and his teacher's daughter both had flaming red hair, they were considered ideal partners and would dance together on these and other occasions.

The star of the film *Nijinsky*, George de la Peña, was also a soloist with American Ballet Theatre, and began ballet because his mother was a pianist at the company school. To avoid leaving him unsupervised, she took him along with her, once he had reached the age of nine. Both George and his father objected to his dancing and, as most boys did, George kept it from his childhood friends. Several years later, George went to the High School for the Performing Arts, where he studied modern dance. The only reason George agreed to this was because after one year of dance he expected to be allowed to transfer to the music department. During the first year, he lost much of his piano technique, and the dance teachers were very eager for him to take up ballet. Since boys are so much in the minority, once a boy begins to study dance, most teachers will try hard to hold on to him. George maintains that he was taken in desperation after doing a short variation that was choreographed especially for him. "Echappé, echappé, changement, changement, one tour en l'air to show my stuff, and I was in." The audition terrified him, since he expected to be faced with a room full of Nureyevs, and it was only after much persuasion that he went. He was relieved to find that there were no Nureyevs, although there were a few boys who were quite proficient.

Pointe work before the age of twelve, or at least ten, normally is not recommended, since the body is insufficiently developed to be able to withstand the strain, and injuries or even permanent physical impairment can occur. Patricia McBride, a principal with the New York City Ballet, and Starr Danias, of the Joffrey Ballet, were both put on pointe while very young. Pat began to study dance when she was seven and was put on pointe almost immediately, and Starr started at the age of six. Although both have become successful professional dancers, Starr feels that poor training in her early years has made her work considerably harder to this day.

Despite the fact that very young girls sometimes incorrectly start pointe work, it is not often that a boy finds himself in the same situation. Jean-Pierre Bonnefous, a former New York City Ballet principal, first took class with his twin sister when he was seven and a half, and he entered the Paris Opera School at ten. He cannot recall whether he liked ballet when he first began to study, but he was the only boy in the class and was put on pointe with all the girls. He was much stronger than they were and would bourrée across the floor, quite unaware of the unusual nature of what he was doing. He says if pointe shoes had been put on his hands as well, he would not have realized there was anything wrong. One of the benefits of pointe work, he now realizes, is that it helped him develop very strong feet.

Gregory Huffman, with the Joffrey Ballet, started his ballet training in a small town in West Virginia, and it was a very lonely time in his life. His childhood acquaintances expected him to be on pointe and would unkindly ask him if he was a ballerina who danced on his "tippy-toes."

Another dancer to be put on pointe too young was American Ballet Theatre principal Martine van Hamel. Martine's father was a diplomat, so the family lived in many different countries, and each time they moved, finding a good ballet teacher was a problem—Indonesia being one such place. Although Martine remembers very little of her classes, she was put on pointe there at the age of seven.

Since ballet training is so rigorous, it is particularly important that a child enjoy it, and when Martine began her classes in Canada at the National Ballet School, she almost lost her enthusiasm for studying. It was there she was introduced to Cecchetti training. The atmosphere was very dry, and nobody ever smiled, or enjoyed dancing. The eventual arrival of an Australian teacher gave new inspiration to Martine, and she began to value the school for its high standards. She later became a member of the National Ballet of Canada, dancing with them for seven years.

Many children have remained fearful as a result of harsh discipline during their early ballet training. There was a time when teachers kept a cane in the ballet studios and would not hesitate to apply it for what was felt to be just cause. Although canes have virtually disappeared, the strictness that went with them still remains in some studios. Steven Caras, for example, has a fear of dancing that dates back to his early teachers. He claims his fear prevents his going onstage and approaching his performances with the spirit he would like to have. His later teachers were more sympathetic, but he remained scared in class and was readily disturbed when one teacher told him he was fat and should not eat during his lunch break. He felt he was living through the ballet *The Lesson* each time he went to class. In this ballet, the teacher drives the pupils so hard that they drop dead one by one. Steve admits that, fortunately, his treatment was less extreme, and he now appreciates the good sides of his early training.

An early teacher usually has a great effect on a dancer's concept of himself, and Maria Calegari, a soloist at the New York City Ballet, is still grateful to her first teacher, who instilled the love of dance into Maria. She was always allowed the freedom to move in her own way and to dance her interpretation of the music.

Another dancer who always found enjoyment in dancing, despite the unkindness of his peers, is Greg Huffman. He started with preballet when he was three because he loved to dance around the house and whenever he had an audience "would move around the floor and smile a lot." Greg is a very coordinated dancer, who moves naturally, so that he feels very comfortable onstage. All of this he attributes to his having begun his training so young.

Teachers' methods are as different as the minds and bodies of the students they are training. Also, students interpret their teacher's instructions differently. The result is that dancers sometimes enter ballet companies without true awareness of how to obtain the most from themselves. Rebecca Wright, formerly a soloist with American Ballet Theatre, says she did not truly understand placement until she was about twenty-four, when she first took company class at the Joffrey Ballet. Although she had always had good teachers, Rebecca realizes there must have been a lack of communication, preventing her from working correctly.

Merle Park, a principal with the Royal Ballet, who started with a good teacher and can appreciate how far technique and teaching methods have developed over the years, wishes training had always been as advanced as today. It is these improvements in training, combined with the demands of the dancer, that have resulted in today's high technical standards.

During both training and professional years, the pressures on a dancer are so great that only the strongest survive. From the day a child starts to take his dancing seriously, he will be infinitely busier than most other children. During his school years, the dancer not only has a full academic schedule but must take a daily ballet class. From the age of about fifteen, he should ideally take more than one class a day, and most advanced-level classes last one and a half hours. Often lack of time precludes a student's taking more than one class a day during the school year, but he will usually compensate for this during vacation periods. Bart Cook was accepted into the School of American Ballet when he was nineteen, and his schedule was so grueling that he would fall asleep between classes. There was not enough time to leave the studios, so he would simply lie down on the dressing-room floor.

Steven Caras was seventeen when he joined the School of American Ballet, after spending one year at the American Ballet Center. Prior to that, he had experienced nothing more exhausting than playing soccer at school and taking two or three ballet classes a week. Suddenly, there was no time in his life for anything but classes. He would rush home to New Jersey each night to take a hot bath so he could move his ankles, and wake up the next morning at six o'clock to hurry back to New York and start again.

Performing in ballets usually causes great excitement in a young child, especially when he is able to appear with an established company, and this normally happens when he takes class at the school run by that company. During his school years, Bart Cook was accepted into the Utah Civic Ballet Company class (now Ballet West) and ultimately danced in his first ballet performance when he appeared in *The Nutcracker* as a mouse. During one of the performances he took a moment to lean over to a nearby mouse to ask who had composed the ballet. He had no idea who Tchaikovsky was at that time, but was overwhelmingly impressed by the beauty of the music and seeing bodies moving around in wonderful patterns. So one young mouse became enthusiastic about great ballet.

It was *The Nutcracker* that first captivated another New York City Ballet principal, Robert Weiss. At the age of five, he was taken to see a performance of the ballet and left with one idea in mind—to play the part of the little prince. He gave no consideration to studying ballet; he wanted only to be in that particular role. Five long years later, he achieved his ambition.

The School of American Ballet has nurtured a great many dancers who are now dancing not only with the New York City Ballet but with other companies throughout the country and in Europe. Gelsey Kirkland, Fernando Bujones, and Patrick Bissell are three outstanding examples. A number of students who finally become well-known dancers are unsure of themselves in the early days, and would probably be the last in line in a group of children asked to step forward to show their capabilities. Patricia McBride once auditioned to appear in *The Nutcracker* and was turned down. She was selected by George Balanchine to join the New York City Ballet after he had watched her in class. In two years she rose from corps de ballet member to principal. He jokingly tells her that if she had had to undergo a formal audition, she would never have been taken into the company. Patricia would be at the back of the class or working somewhere in a corner, but onstage she would come to life, and has always felt at ease during performances. She attributes much of that to having performed in New Jersey prior to entering the School of American Ballet, where she did not have that opportunity. The children at the school have started performing with the company only in recent years.

Bart Cook values the School of American Ballet because before he entered it, he says, he was no more than a "hokey" dancer. Up to that point it had been "all hard sell and show biz—strictly tap and dancing at weddings." Despite this, he is aware of the advantages of those early years as he watches dancers with no experience besides the School of American Ballet who, having entered the company, "take three years before they learn how to smile. Their legs and feet are beautiful but they have frozen faces." Bart had the reverse problem. He had no trouble smiling, but one of the things he had to learn was how to pirouette on axis instead of rotating.

Maria Calegari spent only three years at the School of American Ballet before entering the parent company, so that the bulk of her early training was with other teachers. Maria greatly appreciates those early years, since she believes they formed her as a dancer. "The School of American Ballet deals so technically in certain areas. Students stand at the barre and do all their tendues perfectly, but never when they're twelve do they do thirty-two fouettés. Even if they are done incorrectly, I think you should have the opportunity because it builds a certain strength. It gives you the feeling of moving freely to music, which, after all, is the essence of dance."

Many parents who consider it chic for their child to study ballet take quite a different attitude when they realize that the child is considering it as a career. Adam Lüders, a New York City Ballet principal, Denise Jackson, of the Joffrey Ballet, and Bart Cook all suffered from negative parental reactions.

A former member of the Royal Danish Ballet, Adam was trained at the company school. His father had never wanted him to study ballet, and even as he watched his son progress, he retained his reservations. Now that Adam has been a principal with the New York City Ballet for several years, "he is beginning to change his mind, but after all these years of being against it, he is not going to admit it that easily."

Denise's father would discuss the negative aspects of a ballet dancer's career in the hopes that his daughter would see the light. What would she do if she had a serious injury and her career was finished overnight? If it had not been for Robert Joffrey, who told Denise's parents that she had the talent to become a ballet dancer, her life might have taken a different course. Denise then became a member of Professional Children's School in New York, a school that works around its pupils' schedules and from which countless professional dancers have emerged, such as Gelsey Kirkland and Fernando Bujones.

Bart's parents were not convinced that their son was taking life seriously until he had been with the New York City Ballet for several years. By then they had begun to understand that ballet was a serious career for those who chose to make it so. They realized that, as a member of such an illustrious company, even if he never became rich, he would not starve. "My parents' attitude was always that I was going to get hit by a truck, and I used to tell them that I was just as likely to suffer that if I were a banker." There was no mention then of the risk of being hit by inflation.

Robert Weiss is one of the few dancers who were not only introduced to dance by their parents but were given every encouragement by them. His mother, who had taken class as a child, never fulfilled her ambition to dance professionally, so she wanted her son to have the opportunity. Robert's father was also interested, but Robert, as was to be expected, had the usual difficulties with his peers and did his best to keep his dancing a secret from them.

With ballet now flourishing all over the United States, many begin their studies in small as well as large cities. Some have no desire to leave their homes permanently. They come to New York either to take summer courses to widen their horizons or to study for a year or two before returning home.

Schools associated with regional companies offer far more opportunity for children to perform than do most New York schools. This can have its drawbacks, though, if a child is not taught to keep his capabilities in perspective. If he is overly praised, he can come to New York expecting to conquer the city in a week, and the disappointment resulting from such anticipation can be very painful. Steven Caras learned the hard way. "I really did suffer when I came to New York, because my teachers in New Jersey, and the other kids in the class, kept telling me that I had natural turnout—that I was completely natural in every area I could have wished. Consequently, I waltzed into New York believing them, only to be let down with a jolt. The only aspect that came naturally to me was movement. My 'natural' turnout proved here to be very tight in the hips."

(To help talented students who otherwise would be unable to afford ballet classes, many schools and independent teachers offer scholarships. Most serious students already have an overcrowded schedule, and working scholarships can add considerably more strain.)

While still very young, Dennis Nahat, former principal with American Ballet Theatre and now a director of the Cleveland Ballet, had to wake up at five every Saturday morning so that he could clean the studio between six and nine before taking class himself. Steven Caras would run errands during his days at the American Ballet Center, and remembers once staggering with a large Christmas tree to Robert Joffrey's apartment. Fiona Fairrie, erstwhile member of the Royal Ballet, as a young child was assigned various responsibilities, including feeding her teacher's cat. She remembers that the teacher spent more time in class chiding the children for not having carried out their duties to her satisfaction than she did teaching them how to dance. "How can you expect to be sensitive ballet dancers if you are too selfish to remember to feed the cat?" she would admonish.

Fred Astaire has probably been an inspiration to all people in dance, no matter what form they have studied. His musical playfulness and spontaneity, and the sharp wit he would transmit through his dance, have touched not only dancers but anyone who has ever watched him. Some of the dance world's most notable members appreciate the great contribution he has made to the dance as an art form, rather than having been just an entertainer. Rudolf Nureyev, Mikhail Baryshnikov, George Balanchine, Jerome Robbins, Honi Coles, Bob Fosse, Ginger Rogers, Leslie Caron, and Barrie Chase are some of them.

Lawrence Rhodes danced with both the Joffrey Ballet and the Harkness Ballet and became an international guest artist before retiring. When only nine he was inspired by Fred Astaire and began to study tap dancing. Wanting to follow closely in the footsteps of Fred Astaire was considered acceptable, even desirable, in the forties, and Lawrence began to take class in his home town of Detroit. He first performed at his school's Valentine's Day parade, in response to a request for a boy to volunteer as a partner for the girl who would be doing a tap dance. Lawrence was the only boy to come forward. The little girl taught him a tap dance in her family garage. Since dancers need a resilient floor if they are to dance without injury, the concrete floor must have been quite a shock to their systems, although no doubt it was an effective dancer's equivalent of singing in the bath.

When companies travel, usually they recruit any extras they may need from the city they are visiting, and this can offer exciting opportunities for a young child. Starr Danias appeared onstage with the Bolshoi Ballet when she was only thirteen, during one of the company's visits to New York. They were looking for girls to appear with them in *Ballet School*, originally choreographed by Asaf Messerer especially for the company's tour of the United States in 1962. About two thousand girls were auditioned, of whom only twelve were chosen. When Starr arrived, she was not even sure for which ballet she might be needed, so she went through without the slightest nervousness. Having been accepted, she had her first taste of the ballet world, and it was an experience in the grandest style. She stood in the wings beside Maya Plisetskaya, and then watched the great ballerina do penché arabesque on center stage in *Ballet School*, feeling it must have been the hardest step a dancer could be expected to do. Starr even looks back on an occasion when Galina Ulanova passed by and patted her on the head, as if securing her future in ballet. She also saw Vladimir Vassiliev, Yekaterina Maximova, and Natalia Bessmertnova, "all of them young, upcoming dancers at the time. It was so exciting. I just knew then, standing backstage, that I had to be a professional myself."

Until quite recently, ballerinas were placed in the same category as movie stars, and they were expected to change furs and romances just as frequently. Their lives were considered to be purely glamorous. They were set apart from the public, shrouded in mystery, with few people realizing that their "glamour" consisted of rigorous discipline and hard work, including exercises for which even big-league football players have proved not to have the stamina. Alexandra Danilova was a prima ballerina with the Ballet Russe de Monte Carlo, having left the Soviet Union, where she was trained, a few years after the 1917 Revolution. She recalls her early days, which tended to create the glamorous image. "Before the Russian Revolution, the Imperial Ballet School was financed strictly on the czar's personal capital, and Alexander III, the father of Nicholas II, took a particular interest in the school and sometimes would come and have supper with the girls. He was really fatherly. In those days, and later when I was there, I think there were only about forty girls, so it was very personal. Now that it is supported by the government, it is very much larger. I was never presented to the czar, but we often had the chance to go to the Maryinsky Theatre to see either the Mikhailski French Theatre or the ballet, and we enjoyed the splendor of the magnificent boxes. I was very little at the time, and also very naughty, and therefore not very popular with the directrice of the school. Instead of being allowed to go to the ballet, most of the time I was sent to other performances. However, at Christmas, and every year on the czarina's birthday, we all went to the ballet. On the latter occasion we would receive a special, tasty dinner, and each one of us would be presented with a box of chocolates."

Having trained at the Conservatoire National in Paris, Leslie Caron spent the early part of her career as a ballet dancer, before making movies. She was fortunate enough to have studied with some of the best teachers in Paris at the time, including Alexandre Volanine, one of Anna Pavlova's last partners. Students from the Conservatoire National were usually accepted into the Paris Opera, but Leslie's mother, who had been a ballet dancer, convinced her that she would be happier with the Roland Petit Company. Maybe instinctively she was searching for an excuse to leave the Conservatoire, but it finally happened for a most unlikely reason. All the girls in the school were forced to wear the same hairstyle. "There was such regimentation about it, and the whole principle caused me a great deal of annoyance. I wanted to look more like a classical dancer—like Pavlova with a bandeau. This being the forties, they wanted all the dancers to have a chignon, way up on the head, essentially Esther Williams's style, which I considered very vulgar for a ballet dancer. I wanted none of it, and I left the school just for that reason."

After leaving the Conservatoire National, Leslie Caron started to take class at the school where the Roland Petit Company studied. The first day she was there, Roland Petit invited her to become a member of his company—the start of a rewarding career.

2

Classes

$\mathcal{A}$s the hour approached noon, dancers moved along the lengthy corridor that led to the main rehearsal studio at the Kennedy Center, Washington. It was mid-December, and the American Ballet Theatre was just completing the second week of its four-week visit to the city.

Entering the room, the dancers came across others who had arrived before them, who were doing their own preclass warm-up exercises. One or two were at the barre, and others were lying on the floor, changing positions with great agility as they slowly stretched their legs and backs. Within a matter of minutes, the number of dancers increased so rapidly that they had difficulty finding adequate space in which to work. Portable barres were pulled into the middle of the room, and as ballet master Michael Lland arrived to take class, there was instantaneous organization as each dancer took the position for the first exercise. They stood as erect as a regiment of tin soldiers, the turned-out feet giving the only clue to their pursuit.

Mr. Lland started slowly. The stage at the Kennedy Center is notoriously hard for dancers, lacking the resilience needed to keep injuries to a minimum. Many dancers were sore all over, and looked tired. The company was eased through slow pliés, and many serious expressions were reflected in the mirrors. As the exercises progressed, the dancers moved their arms appropriately, some inclining their heads as they watched themselves in the mirror, others preferring not to watch themselves at all.

Outwardly, it was just another company class. For one, however, it was his last—December 15, 1978, was the day Ivan Nagy retired. His partners for that evening, with whom he had danced many times throughout his career, were all present—Natalia Makarova, Cynthia Gregory, Gelsey Kirkland, and Marianna Tcherkassky. Miss Makarova worked at an old table that was covered in the piping used to make barres. Miss Kirkland, also in the center of the room, was placed closer to the mirrors. Cynthia Gregory stood a couple of places behind Ivan Nagy—from where they were positioned both were unable to see their own reflections.

A student at the David Howard School of Ballet.

The pianist struck an appropriate chord, with "Auld Lang Syne" as accompaniment to a given combination. It was difficult to forget which day it was. Ivan Nagy was respected as both a fine dancer and a dear friend, and his departure would be felt in varying degrees by each one of them. As "Auld Lang Syne" ended, Mr. Nagy turned to the pianist with a formal bow.

The class continued. Before each combination, Mr. Lland moved the dancers into motion with a simple "Préparation." At one point, a man lay down on the floor and pulled one leg back beside his head. A moment later, Gelsey Kirkland broke rank, lifted one leg onto the barre, and, moving as far away as she could on her standing leg, stretched as widely as possible, always leaning against the up-held leg for maximum extension. Natalia Makarova worked her feet beautifully. At the end of the barre exercises, Ivan Nagy completed the final combination with perfect control. Although he was unable to see himself in the mirror, from the other side of the room his image was reflected in it.

The barre exercises over, each dancer took a moment to himself before work began in the center of the floor. Several girls slipped behind the barres and, leaning against the walls, tied themselves in various forms of knots to make themselves more pliable. Away from the barre, Miss Kirkland extended her leg up behind her ear, and Ivan Nagy rested for a moment. Patrick Bissell, after working, yawned, crossed the floor, gave a bear hug to one of the girls, and engaged her in a brief conversation. Shoes squeaked as dancers worked; some went to the rosin box, rubbing each shoe separately in the sticky substance that helps prevent slipping. Natalia Makarova limbered her arms and stretched her neck muscles. That night, in the gala performance, she was to dance in the pas de deux from Act II of *Swan Lake*.

Mr. Lland moved the company onto the floor. "Stretch as you like, every-body." Then, addressing the pianist, he continued: "Give me something nice—not a show tune." After sitting for a moment, Ivan Nagy lay down on the floor and pulled his knees back against his chest. As the barres were moved from the center, he conversed with Cynthia Gregory. There was a low hum of conversation throughout the room. The company was then divided into two groups so that they would not be crowded as they worked in the center.

Despite the relaxed atmosphere that pervaded the studio, there was nothing easy about the way the dancers were working. They seemed powered by inex-haustible energy. Sweat ran down faces and necks, and wet patches appeared on tights and leotards. Many removed extra layers of clothing. Underneath her track suit Miss Makarova wore pink leg warmers over black tights and leotards. She had a cross around her neck, and a scarf was tied gypsy-style around her head. Ivan Nagy was in off-white, also with pink leg warmers, and the familiar Indian scarf around his head.

As work recommenced, Patrick Bissell turned in endless pirouettes, winding slowly to a halt. Seconds later, Cynthia Gregory did the same. Natalia Makarova looked on, her head to one side. Mr. Lland gave instructions from a chair placed at the center of the mirrored wall, in which his back was reflected. The music continued and dancers whirled through pirouettes, the loud squeaking of their shoes heard above the sound of the piano as they spun.

Mr. Lland rose to his feet to show a combination, and Ivan Nagy marked it

David Cuevas, Michelle Benesh, Cynthia Harvey, and Kim Highton await the beginning of an American Ballet Theatre class.

American Ballet Theatre members taking a stretch during class. Gelsey Kirkland is in profile.

Bruce Padgett, left, and Debra Austin, right, warming up before class with the New York City Ballet. (Miss Austin is now a member of the Zurich Ballet.)

with his hands in a mannerism, often used by dancers, that closely resembles knitting. "Is that clear, everybody?" queried Mr. Lland. There was silence. "No? It doesn't show in your faces." Despite the lack of verbal response, the dancers demonstrated that they had grasped the combination physically. Later, as dancers were stretching out at the barre between movements, Mr. Lland continued: "Let's get the blood into our feet a little more, so that jumping will be easier." There was laughter as Miss Makarova announced softly that the blood did not go to her feet.

The class started to thin out as some moved on to rehearsals. Mr. Lland called the dancers onto the floor for the révérence, or bow. One and a half hours after it had started, the work was completed, and Mr. Lland received the usual applause from the remaining dancers before they went their separate ways.

Even after many years as a professional, a ballet dancer still needs a teacher.

The most famous still take class daily, except during vacation, and then they will usually not allow more than a few days to pass without at least doing barre exercises. Being athletes, they need to keep their bodies in peak physical condition, which requires grueling, incessant hard work. Anthony Dowell says, "I wouldn't leave two days before a performance without taking class. In the early days of my career I used to hear the same thing from more experienced dancers, and I could never understand them. Now I realize the benefits of keeping the machine oiled. It's not a case of being dedicated, but I think that as the years go by it makes sense. Also, you feel better for the rest of the day."

Barre exercises are used by professional dancers to warm up the body and work on placement and technique. The length of these exercises varies, depending on the school and the teacher, and may last from fifteen to forty-five minutes. When the dancers move away from the barres to do center work, they begin with the adagio (slow) movements, and the tempo builds gradually to the strenuous

Lauren Hauser of the New York City Ballet warming up before class.

Rebecca Wright during American Ballet Theatre class.

jumps, beats, and fast turns (allegro). Certain teachers include floor exercises in their classes, which are very popular with some dancers because they give a clear sense of alignment and there is little likelihood of injury.

A trained dancer basically takes class for one of two reasons, depending on whether he is performing. Out of season, he uses class to improve his technique. When he is appearing regularly onstage, he attends class to warm up the body before rehearsing or performing. While a certain amount of pressure is removed in studying during performance time, bad habits can creep in during the course of a season. There is so much for a dancer to keep in mind—correct positioning, flow of movement, the music, acting in the story ballets—that something will

Gelsey Kirkland, below, and Ivan Nagy, below right and facing page, in class with American Ballet Theatre.

probably be forgotten. An arm may be used wrongly in a pirouette, or the raised foot will sink too low. Once a dancer reaches a certain stage of experience, artistry, and technique, there is a level he might not go below, but as Anthony Dowell states, "That's not good enough for oneself; one strives to be at the peak all the time, and one just isn't."

Dancers can never relax, and during a heavy season they will probably depend on their teachers most of all, for they must concentrate on the basics. It is not unusual to see a professional studying at a beginners' class on occasion, since

Ivan Nagy after American Ballet Theatre class with daughter Aniko.

American Ballet Theatre class with Natalia Makarova in foreground.

these classes are the hardest. They must be slow and precise, since it is of paramount importance that a student learn to work correctly from the day he walks into a classroom. Basic exercises are extremely difficult for advanced dancers, and practically impossible for anyone to perfect. So the better dancers become, the more they should concentrate on the simple steps. In a beginners' class professional dancers recognize instantly whether they are in shape, even though they may be performing well. Professionals must guard against tension and a tendency to overwork in a beginners' class, to avoid exhaustion. James Dunne, a former member of the Harkness Ballet Company and the Joffrey Ballet, has experienced this. "In a beginners' class you hold steps because that's how you learn, and how the body feels what is correct. Most of the time [professional] dancers move fast in class as they are preparing their bodies for rehearsals—warming up and preparing the muscles to withstand what they're going to do. A beginners' class is very strenuous." Douglas Wassell, associate teacher at the David Howard School of Ballet, in New York, referred to professional dancers with many years of experience, who "can literally sweat from just standing at the barre, working on pulling up and lifting the body so that the spine is elongated and the dancer is not sitting in the hips."

When dancers are performing, the daily routine may be class at ten or eleven, followed by rehearsal as early as noon. Rehearsal may last for three to four hours, and the performing schedule will vary depending on the dancers' level in a company. Principals will usually dance about three times a week; soloists and corps members, five times or more; and some will dance as many as eight times in six days.

A season is comparable to examination weeks, the dancer's "test" being when he is onstage. During an examination period the student has little time to do more studying and increase his knowledge. During the season the dancer must concentrate so much energy on performances that there is not much left for working on improving technique. As students return to books after tests, so dancers examine their technique after a heavy season. Since performing will show clearly the strong and weak points, they will know where to concentrate their efforts in class.

Improvement is difficult. To reach a higher level it is necessary always to go slightly beyond one's limits, and in doing this a dancer can falter and make mistakes. Those who are self-conscious about their weak points may be too insecure to push themselves, feeling that mistakes make them look ridiculous. This is especially true in company class, where dancers are reluctant to display faulty technique before observers, who could include directors, choreographers,

Natalia Makarova in American Ballet Theatre class.

sponsors, and critics, as well as other dancers. Any or all of these can unnerve the sensitive dancer. This insecurity can cause him to work within his limitations, so that he will look his best. Such working produces negative results in performance. As Rosanna Seravalli, a former soloist with American Ballet Theatre, remarked: "It's fine to cheat in a performance because you must get through it; you can't take a chance on losing your balance. If you cheat in class, though, not only do you not build stamina, but onstage you'll fall apart."

Scott Barnard, ballet master with the Joffrey Ballet, believes companies should keep a watchful eye on their dancers, since the degree of self-discipline needed is almost inhuman. "It's asking too much of dancers who do a difficult performance one night to work their bodies hard again the following morning in order to dance even better that night. Yet, if dancers want long careers it is vital to take daily class. When performing they shorten their careers every day they miss. Also, they cheat. If turns are their forte, they warm up that way. If jumping comes naturally, they jump. They try to avoid whatever is difficult for them. I don't expect them to overwork in class, but they must be intelligent about it. Neither Margot Fonteyn nor Rudolf Nureyev would ever miss class. Nureyev may be out until six in the morning, but he'll be in class at ten. The people with the long careers are those who are sensible about their work, and who are prepared to take advice."

One day, in a men's class, Stanley Williams was teaching students at the School of American Ballet, although two professionals were present—Mikhail Baryshnikov and Robert Weiss. Mr. Williams's classes are difficult to master. At one point he asked the men to do three double arabesque turns in a row. Steps done with one leg out behind the body are the most difficult, generally speaking. Although it is usually easier to do a step in series, rather than once, multiples of certain steps, such as double arabesque turns, are exceedingly difficult. To accomplish three in a row requires technical expertise. Even Mikhail Baryshnikov proved the point. Mr. Williams offered him advice. Still Mr. Baryshnikov was unable to complete the third turn. They talked. He worked. Finally, he succeeded. "Now do you see what I mean?" Mr. Williams asked. The dancer grinned. "No, I don't!" he joked. Later Robert Weiss discussed the incident. "You just wouldn't be expected to do three double arabesque turns in a row onstage, although I'm sure in ten years it will be done." Even Mikhail Baryshnikov must push himself beyond his limits in order to achieve great technical heights. If dancers face new challenges, they can improve their technique; otherwise, it deteriorates.

For this reason, classes with independent teachers can be of great benefit. Most serious schools will not allow unqualified observers to be present, and the teachers can devote more time to the individual dancer, since ballet masters conduct classes and rehearsals, give critical appraisals of performances, and assist with problems. In some cases, such as the New York City Ballet, one of them must also be responsible for working out each day's rehearsal schedule. These duties make it impossible for ballet masters to concentrate much of their time on any one dancer. At the New York City Ballet, which has approximately one hundred dancers, merely working out rehearsal schedules can be a formidable task.

With an understanding teacher, a dancer can gain the confidence to work on his weak points. As he improves technically, his self-confidence grows, and this in turn is reflected in his performances.

There should be mutual trust and respect between dancer and teacher. Each must understand how the other works. It is especially important for a teacher to know when to press a dancer to work harder and when to leave him alone. The old-style image of the ballet teacher was that of a stern-faced individual who drove dancers with militaristic severity. He supposedly walked around the studio, cane in hand, issuing orders above the music, devastating the pupils' egos, and reminding them that success as a ballet dancer could be achieved and maintained only through *verk, verk, verk*. This behavior is typified in the film *Nijinsky*, in which Anton Dolin played the role of Maestro Cecchetti. Today such tactics are rare, and usually teachers take a much more humane approach. It is not unusual to see a teacher restraining professional dancers, since they do tend to drive themselves relentlessly, particularly those who feel they need to build stamina. A teacher will often recommend that dancers take only the warm-up exercises at the barre when they are in the middle of a heavy performance schedule, and persuade them to leave before the class is put through the strenuous jumps.

Even company members have to learn to be independent. Ideally, a company class would incorporate combinations from the day's performance, but since dancers engage in different presentations, this is not possible. One dancer may be performing Antony Tudor's classical choreography, while another will dance a Glen Tetley ballet, requiring a totally different, modern technique. Each dancer must arrange his daily schedule to balance his energies appropriately between class, rehearsals, and performances.

Jean-Pierre Bonnefous sometimes gives company class at the New York City Ballet. "It shouldn't be too hard if they have matinee and evening performances— and most of them do on the weekends. I always give a basic class because they never dance *Sleeping Beauty* for a week, as other companies may do. That would be different, and then I think you should do an appropriate class for two reasons. They should have certain things to work on from the ballet, but also I think it is very important for them to be drawn away from it somewhat, so that they don't become stale out of boredom."

After suffering an injury, dancers are particularly sensitive, and it is an occasion for a teacher with an acute understanding of what they are experiencing. Doubts and fears will be constantly in their minds, especially if the damage is serious. They know that if they wish to perform again, they must work through the pain, always with the risk of miscalculation and further injury. Jean-Pierre Bonnefous suffered agony in class while he was recovering from a serious injury. He tore the ligaments in one of his ankles, and the healing process was slow. "I needed someone who could help me, so I took some very simple classes with David Howard. I really suffered landing from jumps, which made me nervous. It was *so* hard. David taught me to work with my arms up, and that was the answer because it deterred me from holding on to the barre, which I tended to do, having grown accustomed to crutches. I would do part of the exercise with the arms raised, which caused me to keep my body more erect, and I became less afraid and dependent on physical support."

Nancy Raffa, now a corps member with American Ballet Theatre, while in class at the school of Mme Gabriela Taub-Darvash.

Helgi Tomasson, principal of New York City Ballet, in class.

Men sometimes take pointe classes, either to strengthen their feet or in preparation for a comic role. The Ballet Monte Carlo de Trocadero is an all-male company that laughs kindly at the classics. In Sir Frederic Ashton's ballet *The Dream*, choreographed on the Royal Ballet, Bottom appears on pointe, though, being a role danced with the feet turned in, it is much less amusing for the dancer than for the audience. Jimmy Dunne, speaking of a former member of the Joffrey Ballet, Jack Hughes, remarked: "He took pointe classes so that when he danced Bottom he was able to stay up there."

All audiences love to see the bravura performances given by the great virtuoso dancers. Such feats take many years of study and constant practice to maintain the body in the necessary peak condition. In class, dancers work to achieve a balance between strength—for jumping—and flexibility, a combination that is extraordinarily difficult to achieve because the demands on the body are diametrically opposed. Dancers need to be supple to stretch their legs to a hundred and eighty degrees, and stretching exercises are also necessary to maintain the long body line that is currently fashionable.

Men need strength for lifting as well as jumping, and Anthony Dowell talked of the difficulties they face: "In order to lift you must build up the lower back muscles, but the more bulk you have in them, the more difficult it is to raise your leg to the back, so it's a vicious circle."

Debra Austin in New York City Ballet class.

Most members of the American Ballet Theatre, the New York City Ballet, and the Joffrey Ballet have been trained in either the Russian, Cecchetti, or American schools or the Royal Academy of Dance. With regard to teaching styles, the word *American* applies to the different methods used by teachers, who glean what they consider to be the best of the established schools and add their own theories. The Royal Academy is neither a style nor a school, but there is a syllabus and teachers must undergo a three-year training course and obtain certification before being allowed to give instruction. Well-known Danes who perform in this country— Peter Martins, Adam Lüders, Ib Andersen, Peter Schaufuss, and the principal teacher of Ballet West, Toni Lander Marks (a former principal with American Ballet Theatre)—studied the Bournonville style, which is taught only at the Royal Danish Ballet School and Ballet West summer school.

Nowadays, even in classical ballet companies, dancers also work with modern choreographers. Larry Rhodes talked of the difficulties dancers can face if they adhere too rigidly to a particular classical style. "Style is something you put *on* dance. You do it yourself to a certain extent; so does the choreographer, and the period. You need a background of information about the styles, but you don't learn a style. In dancing, you should learn how the body stands and moves, and how to build muscle strength. You should not be thinking how pretty you are when you look under your arm, or how much to flick your wrist when you do a particular movement. It's very simple to move the body slightly, or the head, or shape the arm in a different way. If your body is standing up and working with some freedom out of its center, then putting on a little style is no problem. Yet if you work in a style and don't concentrate on the body itself, you will encounter difficulties, such as only being able to move in one particular way."

At the New York City Ballet, the choreography is almost exclusively that of George Balanchine and Jerome Robbins, and the company has a unique style. This has been developed by George Balanchine and is the accepted "American style." It should not be confused with general American teaching, since the style of the New York City Ballet, which is both fast and intricate and derives from Mr. Balanchine's choreography, is dependent on his continuous presence. For a dancer who is already established and who is not used to the Balanchine style, there can be great difficulties, as explained by Peter Martins: "His teaching is on such a high level that the majority of dancers can't even comprehend it—and it's not very easy on the body. Most of them like to feel comfortable after their classes, and with his you don't. Some even say he's not a good teacher, and certainly he is unconventional. On the other hand, I think he's probably the best teacher who ever lived, on a different level. But he's hard to comprehend. It took me five years to understand what was going on. And the body hurts everywhere—in ways that you didn't realize it could. I used to study with Vera Volkova [renowned Russian teacher], who gave very good ABCs. After class I'd feel as if I'd had a two-hour massage, but she was not a choreographer. Mr. Balanchine experiments with you. Working to reach higher levels has never been comfortable, in my experience, but you take the finely tuned body you get from Volkova's class and then give it the rough Balanchine exposure. Then you bring it back and fine-tune it again. It's like a piano—you have to tune it continuously. You have to know your body and exactly how much it can take."

Kay Mazzo, a former principal with the company, experienced her own difficulties in Mr. Balanchine's classes: "I don't think he really cares about your method as long as you do the steps. I've watched him work with boys on double tours. He knows exactly where the problem is when something is wrong, but in his classes—which are enormous—he's more of a coach, showing people his technique, how to do steps and move like lightning. It can be hard taking his classes when you are younger. When I first came into the company, at sixteen, they depressed me so much. I suffered from lack of personal attention because of the size. I stopped going and I couldn't return. I felt terrible." It was a while before Kay worked up the courage to go back.

Although Bart Cook would sometimes miss class, he was always driven by an ideal. He had an image in his mind—but occasionally an incident would bring him down to earth. Once, during his first year with the New York City Ballet, the company went to the Soviet Union. They went to a class at the Vaganova Ballet School studios in Leningrad, which, in the old European style, had a raked floor. All the Kirov teachers were present to watch the ballet class. At one point, Mr. Balanchine gave the men double tours, jetés, and beats that Bart had never remembered doing in Mr. Balanchine's class. He did not realize that dancers were expected to study them independently. Apparently nobody had done this, for the men stumbled. Bart's ideal was shaken. He realized he must learn the steps, by working on them regularly in his own time, to avoid such embarrassment in the future.

After a while with the New York City Ballet, dancers begin to understand Mr. Balanchine. As principal Merrill Ashley explained: "He expects you to have a solid foundation and then he builds a house. If a dancer comes into the company with a foundation of sand, when he builds on it, the house stands for a while and then starts crumbling. He also believes that dancers should not become dependent on their teachers, because this can be devastating in moments of crisis. If their coach is not there, they completely fall apart, and take the attitude that they cannot dance. It's frightening."

Mr. Balanchine is also extremely concerned about his ideas being communicated, as Maria Calegari has learned. "The School of American Ballet claims to teach his way, but they don't quite get the essence. Sometimes they confuse his theories in practice. He likes dancers to leave their heels off the floor when landing from a jump, and teachers at the school picked this up from watching his classes. Immediately, they started teaching all the students to do this, and it is very dangerous if not taught properly because the Achilles tendon shortens. Mr. Balanchine wanted to teach people not to land hard, but to go through the foot and come down gradually. He means the space to be as fine as a sheet of paper, not the width of a book."

Professional dancers go to class dressed in different ways, and there are as many variations in ballet fashions as there are personalities. Many wear leg warmers, or at least ankle warmers, and extra garments on the upper part of the body, for they all help to retain the heat produced by the working muscles. Those made of a fabric that allows air to circulate around the body are practical, and these garments are now generally replacing the plastic pants, once so prevalent in studios.

Since dancers are in class to work rather than consciously set fashions in ballet wear, outfits are thrown together. Generally, they wear subdued colors, as these are preferred by teachers and ballet masters, because they are easier on the eye, but runs in tights, holes in leg warmers, and clothes held together precariously are omnipresent.

The outfits worn by dancers can indicate their mood and how they see themselves on any particular day. If they are not feeling good about themselves they will cover up as much as possible. Leotards and tights hide nothing, so they may wear dark colors and even extra clothing to avoid facing in the mirror whatever it is that displeases them. For professional dancers extra clothing is not really a disadvantage, since a teacher recognizes body line under added layers by the way dancers move. A teacher also respects that dancers need to feel good in order to give their best. If that means covering up to some extent, the teacher will make allowances. However, if dancers constantly use extra clothing as a crutch, the long-term effects are usually negative. If they wear ankle warmers only to compensate for heavy thighs, they are shying away from the root of the problem. If girls consistently wear practice skirts because they are putting on weight around the hips, the same is also true. It only becomes more demoralizing when the costume goes on, and later the stage lighting, for then everything can be seen. Even a long tutu, which has several layers of net, will emphasize rather than detract from any extra weight around the middle.

Martine van Hamel prefers not to wear a practice tutu unless her partner wishes it, since she feels the impact that much more strongly when she finally appears onstage.

If dancers wear sweat pants because they have difficulty straightening their knees in arabesque, they will not learn how to create the illusion that the raised leg appears straighter than it is.

Natalia Makarova and Ivan Nagy during an American Ballet Theatre class break on the day of Mr. Nagy's retirement.

It is interesting to note that the classical (or short) tutu was orginally designed in the 1880s by Italian ballerinas who needed a skirt that would expose their legs as well as enable them to execute their difficult steps. The romantic tutu, which reaches anywhere from below the knees to the ankles, was introduced by Maria Taglioni for the first romantic ballet, *La Sylphide*, in 1832.

Footwear varies from old, discolored ballet slippers to brand-new, shiny satin pointe shoes. It is obvious from watching the girls break in new pairs that the latter will be short-lived. Each has her own ritual. One may sit in a corner of the studio, straddle-legged, unconsciously arching her back for a moment, as she crushes the pointes of a pair of shoes with the heels of her hands, then pulls scissors out of her dance bag to cut the satin from the blunt end of the pointes to help prevent her from slipping when she works. Shoes survive very few wearings. Some girls will go through a pair during a single class, then maybe pour Fabulon or Futura floor polish into the toes before drying them, so they can be worn once or twice more, either in class or at rehearsal.

As they are used, pointe shoes become soaked in sweat. The box (made of buckram, felt, and a special paste) becomes soft, and each girl has her way of drying out her shoes. They may be placed on a radiator or in the oven until dry, although the former treatment makes the pointes brittle. Again, the girls pour in chemicals, which is inadvisable, especially if the dancer has rubbed away skin from her toes. Such substances are not designed to be absorbed into the body, and over prolonged periods they can have harmful effects. As Rebecca Wright learned from her doctor, the chemicals can enter the bloodstream and ultimately accumulate in the liver.

A girl's feet take the most excessive abuse during her years in ballet. From the beginning she must build up calluses for protection when doing pointe work, and there will be very few moments while she is dancing that her feet are not sore. David Howard coaxed Leslie Browne through a series of pirouettes in class one Sunday: "This is where you imagine you have a huge piece of gum in your mouth and you push it against the roof with your tongue as hard as you can, hoping to push the gum through." Leslie, known for her roles in the films *The Turning Point* and *Nijinsky*, stopped turning. She was understandably confused, and her face was motionless. "Then you will forget how much your feet hurt." As Leslie sat to one side later in class and removed her shoes, her red toes gave evidence of great discomfort.

Dancers wear various forms of protection around their toes. Lamb's wool is recommended, although it is by no means used exclusively. Tissue or pieces of thick plastic bag are frequently wound around toes before they are put into pointe shoes.

These shoes are handmade according to a dancer's specifications. Each pair is stamped with the identification of the particular maker, as well as the name of the manufacturer—like the hallmark on a piece of silver, though at present somewhat less of an investment. A dancer rather quaintly refers to the person who makes her pointe shoes as "my maker." This phrase can sound unnerving, even in context, as when before dancing in London with the New York City Ballet, Patricia McBride remarked, "I hope so much to meet my maker while I'm there."

Even though the two may never have met, a dancer usually becomes very dependent on her shoemaker, for correctly fitting shoes are absolutely crucial. A girl needs all her energy and concentration for dancing, and ideally would like to allot minimal time to selecting shoes. Paradoxically, they are one of the greatest headaches in a ballet dancer's career. Natalia Makarova says that out of ten pairs she may find only one satisfactory pair.

By the time dancers become professional, their technique needs only refining, and Nancy Thuesen, who began her career with Joffrey II and more recently has danced with the Elliot Feld Ballet, summarized the essence of their needs in a teacher: "Teachers, I think, should consider what they're training dancers for—which is to dance, not go onstage and do technique. That should be strong, but dancers should be coached to perform, and I think many teachers lose that sense of perspective. A class also should be enjoyable and stimulating, and dancers should never lose the sense of movement. If it is reduced to steps, that's not dancing. Dancers need to experience many different teachers to find which one works for them, and I have found what I need in Mme Darvash [reputed New York teacher]. Not only does she help perfect technique and form, she makes dancers move and change direction. It's awkward and difficult to figure out and make it look good, but that is what you have to do when working for a choreographer. Mme Darvash choreographs, and it shows in her classes. Her combinations are technical chains of steps. She teaches how to come out of one movement with the right energy to go into another and make it work correctly. That isn't learned from 'tombé, pas de bourrée, pirouette,' because that is never done. These are very important qualities in a teacher."

3

Rehearsals

*A*t the New York State Theater, the stage was set for a rehearsal of Jerome Robbins's ballet *Fancy Free,* a section of which was to be danced that evening in a gala performance given by the New York City Ballet. A bar was placed at the back and the barman stood leaning against it. At the left side of the stage stood a table where two girls would sit with three sailors. Once again, each man would try to impress the girls with his physical eloquence and panache, hoping to appeal to them as he danced his variation.

For the moment, the auditorium was quiet and the stage fully lit. Mikhail Baryshnikov was the first to appear. Running across the stage to gather speed, he skated forward on one heel, dragging the other foot behind him as a break, as he worked on a step choreographed for the second sailor's role. He pursued the movements with the enthusiasm of a schoolboy who encounters a patch of ice along the road and, becoming instantly involved, takes his time to slide on it repeatedly, forgetting he has been told to go straight home.

After trying the step several times, he stopped for a moment and joined Mr. Robbins, who had appeared from the wings. The two men moved onstage to work on fine points, each respectful of the other's talent, and fully enjoying the humor of the ballet. Baryshnikov was dressed in a sailor's immaculate summer uniform. Mr. Robbins stood back to take a long look at the dancer's costume and then, moving forward, placed the hat on the back of the dancer's head. Baryshnikov was unsure. "Then I look like Russian sailor!" To avoid being blinded by the lighting, he walked toward the few people in the front row of the auditorium and looked down from the stage. "Better?" he questioned. Having been reassured, he braced his arm muscles. "Everyone wants to look tough and butch." Amused by the situation, he turned to the choreographer. "Anything you want, Jerry."

The lighting was discussed. Baryshnikov asked for the table to be moved farther forward to the first wing. The rehearsal pianist then accompanied him as he worked through the opening passages of his part. Peter Martins arrived and dropped his hat on the table. "Don't you love it?" Baryshnikov asked, pausing for a moment. "Three sailors—one Russian, one Danish, and one half Czech, half French." The final description fit Jean-Pierre Frohlich, the dancer who would complete the trio. Mr. Robbins placed Peter Martins's hat on the front of his head, and he stuck his nose in the air. "I can't see a thing, Jerry," he said, curling his upper lip as he used one end of his tie to make a mustache. His hat was adjusted and he began working on his steps.

As he stood to one side, Baryshnikov watched intently. Next to him was Jerome Robbins smoking a cigarette, his face expressionless, lost in thought as he fixed his eyes on Peter Martins, who was working to perfect his movements.

Jean-Pierre Frohlich then entered. Walking onstage, he sat down and spun around several times, displaying one of his movements, and dirtying the seat of his white pants as he did so.

The dancers went through their steps again and again before the stage was cleared for a complete run-through, each fully aware of what was needed in his role if he was to convince not only the two girls, Sara Leland and Stephanie Saland, but the entire audience, that his was the superior performance. The parts, though short, are demanding, and each man was spurred on by the whistles and cheers he received. As the rehearsal ended, Mikhail Baryshnikov and Peter Martins threw down their hats, and the three dancers stopped to catch their breath.

Before the day of a dress rehearsal, a ballet must be worked on for many weeks, or even months, both in the studio and onstage. For *Swan Lake, The Sleeping Beauty,* and other full-length ballets, principals and soloists rehearse with their partners and also work on their variations individually. The corps de ballet is initially rehearsed together, then later the principals and soloists work with them in the appropriate sections, act by act. A young company member who is dancing a principal role for the first time faces major problems, since he rarely receives a complete stage rehearsal. If he happens to be studying a role at a time when stage rehearsals are being held for the first cast, a dancer chosen for the second or third cast frequently dances behind the principal whose role he is dancing. Stage crews and musicians are so great an expense that companies must keep such rehearsals to a minimum, and for this reason, with the exception of dress rehearsals, a pianist substitutes for the orchestra.

*Starr Danias of the Joffrey Ballet checks
the rehearsal schedule.*

*Natalia Makarova and Anthony Dowell
rehearsing for Mikhail Baryshnikov's production of
Don Quixote for American Ballet Theatre.*

Denise Jackson of the Joffrey Ballet in rehearsal.

*Natalia Makarova and Anthony Dowell enjoy a
moment's light relief during a rehearsal
of Don Quixote.*

Dress rehearsals are often considered expendable for traditional, full-length ballets that have been in the repertoire for a long time, and young soloists are expected to work their way into roles in the course of their performances. The problems that must be faced are many, and dancers can initially become very disillusioned and only after some time start to feel any degree of confidence.

Dancers' entire careers may depend on how they perform their first principal role. The pressure on them is excessive during this time, for without a dress rehearsal, or often even a technical stage rehearsal, they will not be accustomed to the lighting or how to adapt their movements to the size of the stage. Possibly the most crucial aspect and the greatest ordeal is the pacing of the role. If performers start with too much energy, they may well lose their stamina before the end of a ballet. Occasionally they may suffer muscle cramps or other problems that will prevent their continuing to the end.

A soloist must study a principal role thoroughly, for portraying the role of Juliet or Giselle, Romeo or Albrecht, or others of equal prominence, requires significantly more than learning the steps. Young dancers will try to work closely with long-established principals, studying them for hours and turning to them for advice on all levels. Acting is a very important aspect of ballet, and Gelsey Kirkland and soloist Gregory Osborne are two dancers who work with private coaches. Mr. Osborne even studied acting when working on his role in *Etudes,* an abstract ballet requiring immaculate technique. Dancers may read books, the critics, and studies of characterization and look at photographs, films, and stage sets. Performing roles continuously is how dancers progressively develop their artistry.

Like classes, rehearsals are always a necessity, even for the most illustrious performers, who work on subtleties of movement and characterization.

As choreographers are in the process of setting ballets, they supervise the rehearsals. Depending on the way they work, they may like to create solely in the presence of the dancer or dancers on whom the ballet is being set. If a ballet master is not present at this time, he will begin to attend rehearsals once steps have been worked out, although many choreographers will continuously make changes, not only before the premiere but whenever they are working with a particular ballet. Ballet masters, who have always danced, and may be very familiar with a particular work, can contribute significantly to a rehearsal. If a certain step or movement is not working as dancers return to a ballet after a period of time, ballet masters may recall that originally counts to the music or relative positioning between partners was different, and adjust details so that dancers and music are more in harmony.

*American Ballet Theatre
principals Martine van Hamel and
Patrick Bissell rehearsing Natalia
Makarova's staging of*
La Bayadère.

The way a rehearsal is conducted depends entirely on the individual company, its size, and financial resources as to how sophisticated a rehearsal staff it needs or can maintain. Although traditionally rehearsal schedules are worked out by the stage manager, in large companies this is not feasible. At the American Ballet Theatre, the director decides what needs to be rehearsed and the schedule is worked out. As principals and soloists regularly have special requirements, they write them on slips of paper, from which an order is established. Then the schedule is given to régisseur général Richard Tanner, who double-checks to see that there is no duplication. If a principal has requested a specific rehearsal, the régisseur must make certain that it has not been scheduled at a time when that dancer is required to be elsewhere. He must also see that no pianist is given dual rehearsals, that scores are available as needed, and that tapes are sent to the studios where they are required. Tapes are necessary either when a pianist is unavailable or when the music could not otherwise be rendered properly, such as with certain percussive compositions used by choreographer Glen Tetley. The régisseur must work out the schedule in such a way as to avoid overtime, wherever possible, and ensure dancers are given the breaks required by the union. Occasionally overtime is inevitable, such as during the spring of 1980. The company presented its Fortieth Anniversary Gala on May 4 and on May 21 gave the world premiere of its production of the full-length *La Bayadère*, never before seen outside the Soviet Union.

Once a rehearsal schedule is completed, it is typed and must be distributed and pinned on the appropriate notice boards. One of the conditions agreed to in

American Ballet Theatre's 1979 contract was that the schedule be made available to the dancers one week in advance during a rehearsal period and four days ahead in performance weeks, instead of the one day that had previously been customary.

The schedule is studied also by the stage manager, music director, and associate conductor. The stage manager attends whenever a full rehearsal of a new ballet is indicated, in which there is a run-through involving the entire cast. He goes to such rehearsals of other ballets only if they have been out of the repertoire for some time. A conductor attends principals' rehearsals in the early stages, since he must mark his score according to their requirements and those of the choreographer, where relevant. He will also attend corps rehearsals, as he must know how they are being rehearsed. Occasionally the choreographer will make a point that is unmusical, and then he and the conductor must compromise.

The conductor must also coordinate with the stage manager. John Lanchbery, former music director at American Ballet Theatre, orchestrated Ludwig Minkus's score for that company's production of *La Bayadère*, and in the process needed to work out certain points with Jerry Rice, the stage manager at that time. In the first act there are three scene changes, during which the orchestra continues playing.

Martine van Hamel rehearsing Natalia Makarova's staging of La Bayadère.

Fernando Bujones, American Ballet Theatre principal, in rehearsal.

Since he had planned reprises for this, Mr. Lanchbery needed to know the length of each scene change to establish how many minutes of music would be needed.

Lighting designers have individual ways of working, but a designer usually does his initial planning on paper, after having seen either the set design or set models, if they are provided. He attends the technical rehearsals, at which he makes changes continuously. During these rehearsals he sits at a makeshift desk that is set about halfway back in the center of the orchestra, from which he can communicate through a headset or telephone with the stage manager and electricians. A choreographer or director uses a microphone to talk to dancers and stagehands up on the stage.

A lighting designer usually remains with a ballet through opening night; during the performance he sits at the back of the auditorium with the electricians, wearing a headset. Company members and management personnel make use of the soundproof viewing rooms in the few theatres that have them. The lighting designer will frequently make changes up to the opening-night performance, and sometimes afterward.

American Ballet Theatre owns its lighting equipment, which travels everywhere with the company. It is used even at the Metropolitan Opera House, since the equipment is the most efficient and sophisticated available. It is computerized to the extent that when the stage manager gives instructions to the various electricians, the flick of a switch will change as many lights as it is programmed to change.

When the stage manager has all the necessary technical details, he must write his script. Like all stage managers, especially with a company the size of American Ballet Theatre, which appears in the largest auditoriums, he is under tremendous pressure, for he is ultimately responsible for the smooth running of a performance. If a mistake is made there is the risk of lack of coordination. Not only does he control the stage crew, which at American Ballet Theatre is divided into three groups—electrical, props, and carpentry—but he must tie in everything with the conductor. Should he need to attract the conductor's attention while he is in the pit, there is a red light on the podium for the purpose. Since the conductor cannot wear a headset, if necessary the stage manager sends a message with his assistant, who runs into the pit during the performance. In a rehearsal, stage manager and conductor call out to each other over the orchestra pit if they need to communicate.

On the occasion of American Ballet Theatre's Fortieth Anniversary Gala, the script was especially complicated. Since the gala was to celebrate the company's forty years in existence, as well as to honor Lucia Chase and Oliver Smith, co-

GISELLE - FRACCI NUREYEV

BACKDROP

ROCK & CROSS DR   MYRTA CROSS UR
LILLIES OFF L-R   ALBRECHT FLOWERS UL

MUSIC

NUREYEV ENTERS UL   *#2 BR & FR P/U USOP*

X TO GRAVE DR

FRACCI ENTERS DR   *#2 BR & FR P/U DSP*

FRACCI IN & OUT   *LITES Q 23·1 ⑧*

PAS DE DEUX   *WARN #3 FR P/U MYRTA USP DIAGONAL*

THEY EXIT DR

MYRTA & GIRLS IN UR FOR DIAGONAL   *#3 FR - LITES Q 23·1 ⑧*

NUREYEV IN UR   *# 2 BR & FR*

NUREYEV PLEADS

NUREYEV VARIATION

NUREYEV DIES   *WARN # BR & FR*

GISELLE IN UR TO MYRTA   *# 1 BR & FR*

FRACCI VARIATION

NUREYEV JOINS

SHE JETES OFF DR

NUREYEV 2nd VARIATION

CORPS X'ING

HE RUNS UR (MAY EXIT)

    RETURNS FROM UR DIAGONAL TO MYRTA

    X TO UL

    CCI IN UL (OR UR)   *BR & FR*

A page of stage manager Jerry Rice's lighting script of the American Ballet Theatre's Fortieth Anniversary Gala Performance on May 4, 1980. It shows an excerpt from Giselle, Act II, with Carla Fracci in the title role and Rudolf Nureyev as Albrecht.

founders of the company, whose final season it was as co-directors, numerous stars were appearing, and the evening included slides with a voice-over covering the company's history. The slides and the vocal script arrived only on the morning of the gala—thirty minutes before the technical rehearsal was due to begin. Several of the dancers arrived in New York that morning also, and some did not like the order in which they were set to appear in the printed program. These combined problems meant that stage manager, Jerry Rice, could write his script only on the day of the gala. It was a day of exceptional pressures for all concerned, since stage rehearsals continued until five-thirty. Dancers and technical men who had been on their feet all day had to be ready for a seven-thirty curtain. Alexander Godunov talked of the pressures that a dancer is under, and said that no matter how hard a day has been, "when the curtain goes up you must go onstage looking as if you have just had a long rest."

One imagines the daily operation and moving of Louis XIV's court to have been comparatively simple, when watching the planning and organization that are necessary to bring an American Ballet Theatre performance to the stage.

The stage crew must take their lead totally from the stage manager. If they receive a direction contrary to what they might expect, they must assume a change has been made. However, every member of the stage crew must be constantly alert, because there are occasions when one of them must act swiftly to prevent an accident. When Peter Breuer appeared in a particular performance of *Swan Lake* with the company, Mr. Rice had not been able to attend the third-act rehearsal. At the moment when the Black Swan, Odile, exits from the back of the stage with the Baron von Rothbart—the pair having tricked Prince Siegfried into declaring that he wishes to marry Odile, thus betraying Odette—there is a puff of white smoke, and the two evildoers disappear behind the cloud. Normally, the prince does not run to the steps at the back of the stage, but Mr. Breuer did so. Not expecting this, Mr. Rice cued the appropriate crew member to set off the flash pot. This is a strip of gunpowder that, Mr. Rice said, makes no noise as it ignites, simply because it is not enclosed, but he added that it is extremely dangerous. Had the flash pot gone off, it would have done so in Mr. Breuer's face, so the propman did not set off the gunpowder. It is not unusual for a dancer to make a slight change, despite the fact that the stage manager works from his script. Something as seemingly insignificant as entering or exiting through a different wing can require a lighting change.

Ballet is currently recorded by one of two systems in the Western world, Labanotation, devised by Rudolf von Laban in 1928, and Benesh Notation, which

Cynthia Gregory and Fernando Bujones, American Ballet Theatre principals, rehearsing the pas de deux from the black act in Swan Lake.

has been in use only since 1955. A Labanotator and a choreologist are the respective people working with these two systems, and large, comparatively affluent companies may have one or more in residence. Many choreographers like to have their ballets recorded, while others disapprove of notation, since they feel a ballet can become too mechanical or, if set from a score, may not have the right nuances. Consequently, whether or not a Labanotator or choreologist is present at a rehearsal, or is allowed to set ballets from his scores, is the prerogative of the choreographer.*

With so much involved before a ballet is ready for a performance, there is a general feeling among most of the people concerned that there is never enough rehearsal time, and Scott Barnard feels this very strongly. "In an artistic endeavor you can always use more time. You strive constantly for perfection, and that is

* See Chapter 4, "Working with Choreographers," page 63.

impossible to achieve. I have worked on ballets for hours and finally still found aspects that bothered me and that could be improved upon. No dancer is perfect, but if you become complacent and don't aim beyond your limits, you destroy yourself as a performer, and can almost lose the incentive to dance. You will be happy with yourself for a while, and then all of a sudden your dancing becomes unimportant. Considering all the crises that continue until the last minute, I am amazed that there is ever such a thing as a performance."

Robert Joffrey has a reputation among his dancers for insisting on adequate rehearsal time before a ballet reaches the stage. The company is known for its varied repertoire, which not only includes the ballets of Robert Joffrey and resident choreographer Gerald Arpino, but others by some of the world's leading

Anthony Dowell rehearsing Les Sylphides *with American Ballet Theatre soloists Cynthia Harvey and Jolinda Menendez.*

Anthony Dowell and Cynthia Harvey of American Ballet Theatre rehearsing Les Sylphides.

Anthony Dowell rehearsing Les Sylphides *with* *American Ballet Theatre.*

choreographers, among them Sir Frederic Ashton, John Cranko, Agnes de Mille, Léonide Massine, and Kurt Jooss.

Joffrey Ballet members are not categorized, although certain dancers are known for their principal roles. One of them, Greg Huffman, talked about rehearsals. "I think when we perform not many mistakes are made—although I don't wish to speak against other companies. It is very important to make sure everyone knows exactly what he has to do in a performance, because you can destroy a whole movement if something disastrous happens—if two people collide, or one person is up while everyone else is down."

Rarely do dancers feel they are given too much rehearsal time, but this can occur during prolonged rehearsal periods if dancers are working on ballets in which they have performed extensively. If a role is overworked, it can lose some of its freshness and become stale. If steps become too set on a dancer, the element of surprise is lost and a performance can become too predictable. Martine van Hamel spoke also of some of the frustrations that can occur in a lengthy rehearsal period during which time there are no performances. "I think we each have to find our own way within the amount of time we have. Before some of the fall seasons we have rehearsed for about ten weeks, and the first six weeks, to me, may not be very interesting. I tend to pressure myself at the end; it's hard to avoid. We all have our unique ways of preparing for the final.

"Depending on how you work, and who with, sometimes I think you can achieve more in half an hour than in three hours of rehearsing. I tend to work better in the last couple of weeks, because there is a pattern, a way of working up to a performance. You don't have to be in top shape for ten weeks if you're not onstage. It's impossible. I cannot build up adequate strength until I'm close to a performance. Before that it goes in waves.

"When you're rehearsing a new role, the way of working is very fragmented, and does not flow like a complete run-through. You work on different aspects of the role, knowing that you're not going to be onstage the next day, but as soon as you're aware that the beginning of the season is coming closer, you start to pick up. To do a two-hour class in the morning is fine, but then you have to spend most of the day at the studios, and you can't work at maximum capacity for that length of time, it's physically impossible. There is a destructive element in having to work for many hours without performing at the end of the day, which for me is physically cleansing. After rehearsing in the morning, it's fulfilling.

"During a rehearsal you mark some parts and do others full-out, so afterward you're gnarled up. I don't like the way my body feels during a rehearsal period. Normally, performing stretches you out. When you warm up beforehand it's like starting a whole new day, except that you've done it all within a few hours!"

If dancers are already familiar with a part, they rehearse before going back into a season simply to recapture it and establish the feeling back in the body, in the same way an actor would restudy his lines.

The lack of an audience at rehearsal is felt by some dancers, and Patrick Bissell is one of them. "I need the presence of an audience, because it's hard for me to let go and perform when I'm in a studio or being filmed. Onstage I feel more comfortable emotionally, because I become much more involved. I tend to hold back slightly in the studios, which is a problem. I don't know why, but sometimes I don't give my all, and that defeats the object, because you must practice gestures and facial expressions, otherwise you arrive onstage with deep feelings that you want to portray but can't because you haven't become accustomed to accompanying them with gestures. It's very important to work on such details, because if you can't convey your emotions to the audience, they won't be able to share your feelings."

Traditionally, rehearsals are conducted by the appropriate company staff, but at the New York City Ballet the principals work on their own. Occasionally they will request the presence of either Mr. Balanchine or Mr. Robbins, but usually only if they encounter difficulties. This is a subject of controversy, even within the company, for some dancers feel insecure when unsupervised. However, Peter Martins, who has danced with many of the world's leading companies, prefers to work without a ballet master. "I feel that dancers should develop the fine points themselves. With the exception of the New York City Ballet, companies pander to their dancers in a most destructive way. Here the principals take care of themselves, and I know sometimes it doesn't look good onstage. Sometimes you can tell. People say we should have rehearsed a little more. On the other hand, it gives it an element of excitement. There is a very desirable atmosphere within the New York City Ballet—the dancers are treated like adults. There is so much more involved than being told to keep your shoulder down or your rear end in. Balanchine and Robbins have such vision that I respect their judgment, but otherwise I cannot stand having someone tell me what to do."

Kay Mazzo did not like to rehearse unsupervised, because turning her head to look in the mirrors meant she had to break the line she was working to achieve. When the time came, she preferred to rehearse onstage, rather than turn her back on the mirrors, because, as she suffers from astigmatism, it was difficult for her to "spot" onstage. The auditorium is black, and lights shine in from both wings, presenting a totally different aura from that of the studio, and affecting all aspects of a performance. When mirrors are available, dancers fix their eyes on their own reflection, whereas in the darkness of the auditorium it is more difficult to establish a focal point.

David Howard recalls an incident when he was a member of the Royal Ballet. The company was performing in Greece in a large amphitheatre. The setting was exquisite but the dancers looked out from the stage into total darkness. At the request of Dame Margot Fonteyn, during a performance of *Swan Lake* Mr. Howard sat in a strategic place at the back of the amphitheatre holding two flashlights so that Dame Margot would be able to spot.

During the first stage rehearsal of a ballet, dancers are usually very disoriented, and many things can go wrong. One of the few advantages to working in the studio, Kay Mazzo feels, is that the main rehearsal hall at the New York State Theater is the same size as the stage.

Principals at the New York City Ballet rehearse on their own mainly because of insufficient time, studio space, and availability of ballet masters, which often prevents coordination of schedules. Either Mr. Balanchine or Mr. Robbins will usually supervise stage rehearsals, and one of the ballet masters must be present in the studios while the corps de ballet is rehearsing. The principals, who request their own rehearsals, are normally accompanied by a pianist, and only if one is not available do they work with tapes. They are given a studio at whatever time it happens to be free. Since the studios are often occupied throughout the day, principals are frequently scheduled to rehearse after six, by which time all other rehearsals must be finished.

Dancers dislike last-minute rehearsals, which most commonly occur when a scheduled performer has been injured. In minor roles, understudies frequently have done minimal work on a part, due to lack of available rehearsal time, although this can occur with a principal in a short ballet. If a company is giving several performances of a particular full-length ballet and a principal is injured, there can be great problems, since partnering may have to be changed, and whoever is chosen to cover the injured dancer will probably have to dance an

Natalia Makarova warming up before a rehearsal with American Ballet Theatre.

New York City Ballet members on stage for rehearsal—from left to right: Toni Bentley, Dana Lewis, Diana White, Melinda Roy, and Leslie Roy.

Nina Fedorova in the wings during a New York City Ballet rehearsal.

extra performance. If more than one performance is affected, then a second principal may be asked to cover.

After the company had given only one of four scheduled performances of *Don Quixote* at the Metropolitan Opera House, an emergency arose one Saturday morning, at the American Ballet Theatre studios. Cynthia Gregory, scheduled to dance that evening with Peter Breuer, had suffered an injury. The previous evening, Martine van Hamel had danced Kitri, partnered by Patrick Bissell, and she had had to leave New York that morning. The other casts due to perform were Cynthia Harvey and Anthony Dowell at the Sunday matinee, and Yoko Ichino and Danilo Radojevic in the evening. The incident presented a dual problem. Should dancers already used to working together dance on the Saturday, and if so, who? Audiences usually buy tickets to see the dancers of their choice in a certain ballet, and the Sunday-afternoon cast could not be expected to do two performances of this particular ballet in so short a time. This left only the Sunday-evening cast.

By this time, Peter Breuer had been rehearsing for three weeks and it seemed that he should be given a chance to perform, especially as the press would be there to see him. As Sunday was to be the occasion of Danilo Radojevic's first performance of the ballet, it would also have put an unreasonable amount of pressure on him if he had had to dance on two consecutive evenings. Yoko Ichino was ultimately scheduled to dance on the Saturday night, leaving only the few hours during the day to be snatched for rehearsal.

That morning Yoko had taken class elsewhere, but then she would be at the studios for her expected rehearsal. Meanwhile, the ballet master for *Don Quixote*, Jurgen Schneider, was changing the schedule wherever necessary. Everybody waited. The tension was high, and to relieve it dancers occupied themselves in various ways, some finding it a moment for humor. A few paced between the two studios, which were filled with activity. In the main studio, Anthony Dowell and Cynthia Harvey worked in earnest. Laughter came from the adjoining studio as Peter Breuer and Danilo Radojevic created their own comedy, bringing people scurrying to the door to see what was causing the amusement. The entertainment over, Danilo left the studio, holding his head in his hands as he remembered suddenly what would be expected of him within thirty-six hours. "My God, what am I doing," he said, coming down to earth. "I must be serious."

Outside the studios, Richard Schafer sat reading the *New York Times*. Gregory Osborne arrived in blue jeans and did not change, for he was to dance the part of the suitor, Gamache, and would not need to be dressed in ballet clothes for the rehearsal. Soloist Janet Shibata paced back and forth in practice clothes, and a corps member, impervious to her surroundings, sat engrossed in a book.

After what seemed like an interminable length of time, the elevator door opened and out stepped Yoko Ichino. Instantly, she was surrounded as several people tried simultaneously to explain to her what had happened in her absence. As Yoko quickly prepared to work, Anthony Dowell and Cynthia Harvey moved into the smaller studio, leaving the larger one free for the many company members involved in the first act of *Don Quixote*.

When they are not required to work during rehearsal, many dancers do not like to stand idly to the side of the studio, and so will select a movement and practice it repeatedly. As Peter Breuer and Yoko Ichino, and those involved with them, were rehearsing, one or two dancers were active in the background. Corps member Peter Fonseca chose fast pirouettes à la seconde, then continued in adagio before finishing in attitude, all of which he executed with perfect control.

During a break between the first and second acts, two girls put on one large T-shirt, and as they started to do steps, the pianist struck up "Me and My Shadow" to complete the entertainment. Danilo ably rehearsed steps from Basil's variation in the drunken scene from Act II of *Don Quixote*, and ballet master Enrique Martinez, who was conducting the rehearsal (he has since left American Ballet Theatre), talked with Peter Breuer and Yoko Ichino.

Throughout the rehearsals, Ludwig Minkus's music drifted from the doors of the two studios, cacophonous where it met. Danilo, bereft of his partner, Yoko, worked alternately in both rooms. Taking a momentary pause, Anthony Dowell left his studio and watched Peter and Yoko as they worked. Later, when the main rehearsal was over, they continued on their own.

During one of the New York City Ballet's July seasons at Saratoga Springs, New York, Merrill Ashley was cast in three ballets that she had never performed or even rehearsed before. One of them, *Union Jack*, she learned in a single day and performed the same night. "I felt fried at the end of it. I spent the whole day learning and rehearsing the ballet. Due to a chronic injury, Suzanne [Farrell] had kept cancelling performances at the last minute for the entire season at the State Theater. That week she had maintained she would be able to do *Union Jack* only; then when the morning of the performance arrived, she realized she would be unable to go on. I was the understudy, but when the ballet had been rehearsed I was injured, so I could not learn it—although it did become familar to me. I had pleaded to be rehearsed, knowing the day would arrive when I would have to perform it, but time passed and nothing was scheduled. The day of the emergency, I rehearsed for five hours, and spent two of those learning the part. There were sections that only Suzanne knew, and she wasn't there to teach them to me. Even Mr. Balanchine couldn't remember them. I was able to do similar steps and he seemed quite happy, since he had not been satisfied with certain of the missing steps in his original choreography. He adapted it to my capabilities, and chose movements I am good at, but he made it so hard! It's a ballet that should be well rehearsed, so that you can get it into your body. The reworking occupied the third hour. Finally, we spent two hours doing complete run-throughs, and then I just kept repeating the ballet during the remainder of the day. It was a benefit performance that night, and the program consisted of *Tricolore, Stars and Stripes*, and *Union Jack*. The only one I did not dance in was the middle one.

"I finished rehearsing about six o'clock and didn't leave the theatre. I stayed there and sewed [elastic and ribbons on] shoes. It was all frantic, and after it was over I just collapsed. Then I had to perform in *Union Jack* the next evening, and I was so afraid I would have forgotten it overnight, I rehearsed the whole ballet over again, and then kept repeating the parts I needed to. The problem after the second day was that although I felt like collapsing, I couldn't." Despite all the effort that is expended on such occasions, sometimes a dancer will never perform in the role again.

When a corps de ballet member does not know a principal role and is chosen to perform it on short notice, it can be a traumatic experience. Elise Flagg, at one time with the New York City Ballet, and currently a principal with the Zurich Ballet, went through this ordeal, and the incident stands out in her mind as having been very frightening. When the New York City Ballet staged a Stravinsky festival, ballet master John Taras choreographed a ballet on Gelsey Kirkland, then still a principal with the company, to *The Song of the Nightingale*. There are two nightingale roles in the ballet, one living, the other mechanical, and Elise had been cast in the second role.

Two days before the premiere, Gelsey Kirkland seriously injured one of her feet during a rehearsal of Jerome Robbins's ballet *Evening Waltzes*. As it was a subscription performance, the company did not want to cancel *The Song of the Nightingale*, and Elise Flagg was chosen to dance in Gelsey Kirkland's place. The most frightening experience she had ever had was learning to perform to the Stravinsky music in so short a time. Unfortunately, because Elise was originally cast in the role of the mechanical nightingale, she had never watched Gelsey do her part. Elise was too busy in the wings putting on the costume, in which she could hardly move. It was so heavy that she found it difficult to walk, and putting it on and taking it off was a lengthy process. Having been scheduled for the part at 10:00 A.M. prior to the day of the performance, Elise "went into total shock" and rushed to the State Theater to meet John Taras. "Later on in the day, Gelsey also came and guided me. I had never listened closely to her music before, and the counts were difficult to learn. Much of it was done in threes, but the steps were hard, because the ballet is very stylized. So we worked—with Gelsey on crutches! I think we rehearsed for six hours, with one hour off in the middle. I was nineteen at the time, and at the end of the day I burst into tears. John was rather stunned, but I couldn't help it. That night I felt the ballet had completely left me, and I was so nervous I could not sleep at all. I called Gelsey, who was very understanding and told me that she would come and work with me again the next day. There is one variation under a spotlight, and I was terrified that my mind would go blank, because I had rushed the part into my head. When the time came for the performance John stood counting in the wings, and I got through the ballet. I was very touched afterward when Kay Mazzo came backstage and told me that I was beautiful and had done a wonderful job. Support from colleagues is so important, particularly during those moments. After that we had time to rehearse."

Elise then talked of how a dancer may struggle with a particular ballet without understanding what is causing the difficulties. At such times it is essential for a dancer to be able to seek out the choreographer, ballet master, or a dancer familar with the role, so that the problems can first be diagnosed and then worked on. While with the New York City Ballet, she danced in *Concerto Barocco*, which she considers to have been her most important role while she was a member of the company. She had been rehearsing her part for three months, and on the day prior to the performance she suddenly became very nervous, wondering how she would be able to dance the ballet. Mr. Balanchine, the choreographer, went to watch her final rehearsal, not realizing how nervous Elise was. He entered the studio with his hands in his pockets, and asked Elise and her partner, Bart

Cook, if they were ready to begin. Elise, who was still tying her shoes, replied that she was not. That task completed, she took time to rub each shoe in rosin. Once the partners started to run through the ballet, Mr. Balanchine made few, important comments with regard to style and timing. *Concerto Barocco* is a very geometric ballet, and there was one step with which Elise had always had difficulty. Mr. Balanchine was able to straighten out the problem as soon as he saw the way the two were working. They had been taught to count in sixes, and Mr. Balanchine recognized immediately that something was wrong. He stopped the dancers, requested the pianist to play the music, and then changed the count from sixes to threes, so that the movements would be slow and free. Counting in sixes was causing the dancers to work too frantically, whereas in threes the body moved more slowly with the music. As Elise said, "We had not been listening to the music to help us through the step. After the rehearsal I wasn't nervous anymore, and Mr. Balanchine was very encouraging. He hugged me and told me that everything would be all right. I was relaxed for the rest of the day. That night the performance went very smoothly and the ballet looked fine."

Bart Cook spoke of rehearsals that take place two hours before the curtain. "You have [what seems like] two minutes in front of the mirror and then you are onstage. In a corps scene you can get by with that very easily, because there is so much movement and several people are involved. There is somebody to guide you every step of the way, even to tell you which foot to start with. Your chief concern in a case like that is just getting through the performance without a disaster."

Despite the advances in training and the superior technical capabilities of today's ballet dancers, there is a serious dearth of proficient coaches to guide the less experienced. As Anton Dolin stated, "We need good dancers to coach, not just to teach how to do entrechat-six." He also talked of the willingness of the great Russian dancers to accept and even request help, whereas he feels today some principal dancers elsewhere are not as open to the constructive criticism that would be in their interest. He spoke specifically of a gala that had been held in Paris for Alicia Alonso, before which he had watched the great principal of the Bolshoi Ballet, Vladimir Vassiliev, being coached by prima ballerina assoluta Galina Ulanova. Normally, the Russians dance as full-out in rehearsals as in performances, and Mme Ulanova was working with him on every subtlety. When he felt unsure of his acting, or specific gestures, Vassiliev would ask for advice. In the performance that night, he performed according to her suggestions.

Former Bolshoi Ballet principal Andrei Kramarevsky, who now teaches at the School of American Ballet, talked of the disadvantages that can occur when a

Mikhail Baryshnikov rehearsing onstage for the ballet Coppelia *for his first performance with the New York City Ballet.*

Mikhail Baryshnikov rehearsing the title role in a stage rehearsal of George Balanchine's Orpheus *with New York City Ballet.*

master of ballet tries to coach his own style into a young dancer, instead of allowing him to develop his own originality. "A teacher must see what the dancer can do, and not what he would like him to be able to do. He must develop a dancer's individuality, according to that dancer's capabilities. Each body is unique and should be developed to its best advantage. Ulanova tried to develop her own style in Yekaterina Maximova when coaching her for *Giselle*. Maximova became aware of the situation and so was able to keep her own uniqueness."

Many young dancers, especially those studying principal roles, would appreciate being able to work with a coach, and very few receive the personal attention they would like. Cynthia Harvey went through a variation that she was to dance as the jealous concubine Gamzatti in *La Bayadère*. David Howard had offered to coach Cynthia in the variation, though this was the first time he had seen it. As the complete ballet had never before been seen outside the Soviet Union, only the "Kingdom of the Shades" scene is universally known to ballet audiences. Since the variation was new to him, Mr. Howard simply gave suggestions he felt would facilitate some of Cynthia's movements. Afterward she spoke of her appreciation. "I am really grateful to David for his assistance. At Ballet Theatre they just don't have the time to coach us individually, and it is so important because a dancer needs that help."

Stars are fortunate in that coaches will take the time to give them personal attention. For example, Natalia Makarova works with Elena Tchernichova, formerly a member of the Kirov Ballet, as well as with David Howard. Anthony Dowell is coached by Michael Somes when dancing with the Royal Ballet, and Jurgen Schneider when appearing with American Ballet Theatre, both men former principals with the Royal Ballet and Stuttgart Ballet, respectively. Michael Somes preceded Rudolf Nureyev as Margot Fonteyn's most frequent partner.

If, as is most common, one dancer learns a part from another, how many "secrets" will be passed on depends on the teacher's generosity. Some will do all they can to eliminate the difficulties a dancer has in working the feel of a new ballet into his body, and are willing to give hints. Others are not so helpful, as Merrill Ashley mentioned. "Frequently you learn a role from a dancer who has done it before you. Some dancers are very generous with their tips, others just show you the steps. Sometimes there are qualified people watching in the studio, but, unfortunately, most of the time they won't offer advice."

When one dancer is learning a role from another, he does it by working from behind the demonstrator. As dancers also frequently learn parts from film, Peter Martins said it would be ideal if films could be shot from behind dancers. Learning from a film taken from the front presents obvious difficulties. "You are constantly having to turn your back to it so that you can watch it over your shoulder to get the steps the right way around."

Staging a choreographer's ballet without his presence is challenging, and carries heavy responsibilities. Sara Leland, a principal with the New York City Ballet, now travels internationally to set the works of both Balanchine and Robbins. "You have to try to see it through the eyes of the choreographer to make sure it has the right 'look.' When I am staging ballets for international companies, or the regional American companies, I tell the dancers the same things as Mr. Balanchine or Mr. Robbins tells us, so that they have not only the ballet, and the sets where appropriate, but the style as well. That is equally important. Since both Balanchine and Robbins have such fine taste, there is usually not much conflict with the people I go to work with. When I go away to stage a ballet, I feel that I have a tremendous responsibility. If I teach the dancers and they don't look right, that's not good enough, and I must see that they wait until they're ready. Generally, I'm sent to companies that have reached a certain level of proficiency, and Mr. Balanchine knows that they're able to do the works. Alternatively, I will go

Peter Martins as the third sailor in Jerome Robbins's Fancy Free *with the New York City Ballet.*

and watch them perform to ensure that they dance well enough to give an adequate representation of a Balanchine or Robbins ballet."

Sara talked about some of the companies she has worked with, including the Ballet Nacional de Cuba. "I think they're a wonderful company. They're well trained and hardworking. As they have that Latin flavor, they are able to do lively ballets to Latin music in a way that we [the New York City Ballet] could never do. They're very sexy and very emotional dancers, and the girls are gorgeous. I staged Jerry's [Jerome Robbins's] ballet *In the Night* for them. The drama was just overpowering, but I loved their interpretation, and I thought Jerry would too. I tried to tone it down slightly to take the *Giselle* out of it. I advised them to take it easily, to keep the ballet simple, and not to perform it like a Greek tragedy."

Ballet is a precise art, and in rehearsal dancers must concentrate on more than learning or polishing steps. Musical phrasing is as important as the choreography, and the more musical the dancer, the more time he will devote to suiting his movements to the music. In essence, he dances the music rather than dancing *to*

*Jean-Pierre Frohlich of the New York City Ballet as the first sailor makes his point in
Jerome Robbins's* Fancy Free . . .

it. In the Soviet institutions great emphasis is placed on this area of training,
because a dancer who is unmusical can be as uninteresting to watch as an equivalent singer or instrumentalist can be to listen to.

Each dancer moves differently and develops his own musical phrasing, and if
the choreographer of a given ballet is available to work with him, he will often
change or adapt steps to a dancer's capabilities. This is customary at the New
York City Ballet, as Mr. Balanchine will not allow the music to be played in any
way other than that intended by the composer.

When a dancer first learns steps, depending on the music he is working with,
he may or may not learn by counting. Either way, once he has learned how the
steps fit the music, he develops his own musical phrasing through repeated rehearsals and performances. Greg Huffman spoke of the importance of allowing
each dancer to work in his own way. "Counts are no longer necessary once you
have become familiar with the music, and that is what is most important. After
you have done a ballet for at least six months, you already know it musically, and

. . . and Mikhail Baryshnikov as the second sailor woos principal dancer Sara Leland.

I hate to be counted through it. 'This happens on six; on five; on one.' What does that mean? I may want to do something on one and a half, or two, and catch up on five. This can cause annoyance, but I dislike it when a ballet master doesn't give you the freedom to do your own phrasing, or objects if you don't reach the place you're supposed to be on the count of two."

John Neumier has choreographed a pas de deux on Natalia Makarova and Anthony Dowell, entitled *Désir*. In an American Ballet Theatre rehearsal one afternoon, ballet master Jurgen Schneider was assisted by choreologist Dora Frankel and the pianist was Robert de Gaetano. The dancers were still learning the music and, as Ms. Frankel commented later, "the Scriabin music is difficult and the dancers were still in the process of feeling comfortable with it, but as it is a pas de deux, they were able to play with the music more than they can when there is a corps involved. Then soloists must do their piece of the puzzle for purely practical reasons, or they can really cause confusion and hit other dancers."

As the rehearsal commenced they decided to work on the second bicycle promenade,* and as the dancers started to move they quickly realized that the pianist was at a different place in the music. They began again, and later stopped for discussion. "For me that's OK," said Mr. Dowell, "but I don't know how it is on pointe—so maybe I should delay it a little." Mr. Schneider and Ms. Frankel rose from their chairs and tried the movements themselves. Eventually the timing was worked out and they continued. The rehearsal proceeded smoothly until a moment arrived when the two dancers became confused by a step and the resultant move was comical. Miss Makarova, putting her head in her hands, leaned against Mr. Dowell. "Natasha is too early in the tombé," announced Mr. Schneider; "she could wait a little and not move so evenly." A short time later, the two dancers paused for a rest. Ms. Makarova yawned, and she and Mr. Dowell walked through a few steps, discussing coordination. Mr. Dowell, known for his ability to move fast, then broke into steps from his variation, darting around the floor and adding a touch of humor. Miss Makarova laughed. The short, crisp steps were amusing. They proceeded to work together again, concentrating hard on their movements. Whenever possible their eyes would dart to the mirror.

The rehearsal nearly over, there was pause for a postmortem, in which details of the hour's work were discussed. Miss Makarova picked up her cup of coffee, which by this time must have been completely cold. Having lit a cigarette, she walked through a few steps from the score with Dora Frankel. Ms. Frankel was trying them herself to see what was causing the difficulty, since steps on paper cannot be completely understood without practical experience. Meanwhile, Mr. Dowell went to the barre and stretched his feet before sinking to the floor to rest and watch Miss Makarova. Almost instantly he was up again, standing in a casual pose, his hands on his hips, to discuss a particular step in relation to the depth of the stage at the Metropolitan Opera House.

Mr. de Gaetano picked up in the score from Mr. Dowell's variation. He began to move and then stopped moments later. The two men talked and then began again. Miss Makarova tied a sweater around her waist and sat on a chair next to Mr. Schneider. "I know he [John Neumier] wants this feeling of unwinding—but while I'm doing a step like that . . ." Mr. Dowell paused to think. He continued and then stopped and asked Mr. de Gaetano to go slightly more slowly, as he felt too rushed. Next Miss Makarova went through her variation, and she found her music too slow. Mr. Dowell put a towel around his shoulders and sat down. Miss Makarova danced full-out, then she slowed. The pace built again, and Ms. Fran-

* The man lifts the girl into the air and she makes cycling movements with her legs.

kel clapped her hands to stop the proceedings. She and Miss Makarova talked. They picked up in the middle, and it took two or three attempts before the exact place could be found in the music, partly because the score had no dancer markings. Ms. Frankel says that usually a rehearsal pianist will mark the score and that sometimes she will offer advice.

The section completed, Miss Makarova stopped. She had to leave to take a massage. There was a decision for a half-hour rehearsal the following day after class so that they could do further work on the pas de deux.

Miss Makarova and Mr. Schneider having left the studio, Mr. Dowell and Ms. Frankel paused for a light discussion with Mr. de Gaetano. There was reference to the pianist's long hair, which he said he was growing for a performance of Gottschalk music in which he would be playing. Ms. Frankel misheard, as her next words indicated. "The Gottschalk show, not the *Gong Show*," clarified Mr. Dowell. "How far would you get before they gonged you?"

Watching a rehearsal closely, one becomes acutely aware of the work required, the difficulties that exist—both physical and emotional—and the fine details that must be worked out, which an audience takes so much for granted. Ivan Nagy summed up the experience for so many dancers by referring to rehearsals as a time of agony.

From just a few feet away, one sees the dancers' chests rise and fall with ever-increasing rapidity, as their bodies require progressively more oxygen to cope with the strain of the work. As one watches the veins stand out on their foreheads and necks, and leotards and tights become wet with sweat, dancers' agony becomes evident. When a studio stands empty after only a few hours of use, the acrid smell that hangs in the air testifies to the athleticism that has taken place—all traces of artistry having departed with the dancers.

When viewing the great artists of the dance, one is struck by their moves, which appear so automatic, yet are accomplished only after years of study. In partnering, if the man does not place his hands correctly around the woman's waist as she pirouettes, he can push her off axis. When learning, a boy has to practice for hours to avoid letting his fingers become caught as the girl turns in his hands, at the same time giving her the support that she needs. When a woman pirouettes, the partner must work in such a way that she does not kick the man when turning. This usually concerns the women more than the men. In a rehearsal some days before he retired, Ivan Nagy worked with Marianna Tcherkassky on the pas de deux from the "Kingdom of the Shades" scene in *La Bayadère*. "Marianna, you don't need to worry about kicking Ivan when you're doing those pirouettes," assured ballet master Michael Lland. Later, Martine van Hamel talked of this technicality. "You very rarely kick a partner, and a lot of the time it's an instinctive reaction to pull away from something rather than doing it full-out and seeing whether you hit the man or not. Usually he says you won't because he sees your leg going by."

Sometimes even remembering to breathe is a problem. After one section of a rehearsal, Marianna Tcherkassky announced that she had been thinking about so many other things that she actually had forgotten to do so.

On certain days rehearsals can go very smoothly, while on other occasions they will be plagued with difficulties that seem insurmountable. Even principals with years of experience are not immune to such problems. Ballet is a complex, athletic art, and, as Ivan Nagy stated, "No aspect of it is mathematical."

With all the details that have to be taken into account, Scott Barnard talked of the pressures that a ballet dancer must learn to take if he is to survive company life. "When new people come into the company, I think some of them must think I'm mean! It's not easy for them. From the first day they must learn to take correction and having someone tell them what is right or wrong—often quite forcefully. If they can't take this, they will never keep their nerve onstage in a new ballet, in costume, and with lights hitting them in the face and a choreographer changing steps until the last minute. A dancer has got to deal with that, and if he can't take pressure initially in class or rehearsal, he's never going to withstand the pressure of performing. Once he gets through a few ballets, then he starts growing. When dancers reach a certain level, like Denise Jackson or Starr [Danias], you can show them certain things at the last moment. The steps would not be there, nor the musicality, but if they're professional enough and sufficiently calm, dancers can give a performance. In rehearsal one even has to think of details such as ensuring a girl's [shoe] ribbons never come out [at the ends]. If they do in rehearsal, they certainly will onstage when they dance, and that's not pretty."

4

Working with Choreographers

Ballet is the most ephemeral of the arts. The classical works of Petipa and Ivanov that still are with us, which include *Swan Lake* and *The Sleeping Beauty*, probably bear little resemblance to the original ballets set by those choreographers. Unlike the music of the great composers, most of which still exists in its original form, the recording of ballet has been less concrete. Notation deals with the human body in motion, but although it is a very specific shorthand, notation varies according to the abilities of the person recording a given choreographer's work.

George Balanchine and Agnes de Mille are two choreographers who have shown reluctance to work with Labanotators or choreologists. The great former ballerina, Dame Alicia Markova, said of notation: "I find it is excellent, but it's without soul. It gives the structure. Then you need the choreographer, I think, to come and give life—put the blood into it and get the heart beating."

When a choreographer sets a ballet, he usually works with specific dancers whose performing abilities he likes. As he is creating, he will work not only to show off the music to its best advantage, but also to bring out a performer's strong points while playing down his weak ones. If he is reviving a ballet after a period of many years, a choreographer may make whatever changes seem appropriate either to contemporize it or to suit the dancer or dancers with whom he is working. When an established choreographer finds a notator he can work well with, the notator will often be called upon to travel with him internationally, an invaluable asset in recording his works. Companies that have a sufficiently large budget may commission a choreographer to choreograph a ballet or to set an existing work on certain dancers in that company. The company may also pay for a notated manuscript of the work, so that they may build a library of ballets. This will enable them, if necessary at a future date, to employ a notator to set a ballet on their dancers, rather than having to always depend on the presence of a choreographer, whose costs often can be prohibitive. Manuscripts also have the advantage of preserving a choreographer's ballets after his death.

Dora Frankel, an expert in Benesh Notation, spent one year with American Ballet Theatre. She was the first resident choreologist to be employed by the company, which up to that time had employed freelance choreologists. A trusted notator of Glen Tetley's ballets, among others, Ms. Frankel is still something of a pioneer in the ballet world. She believes the pressures on a company the size of American Ballet Theatre to keep its repertoire in shape are phenomenal, and says that ballets can start to look underrehearsed and "nothing but a mess" unless the scores are used.

Since ballets have mainly been handed down through dancers and ballet masters, who know them well, it is very easy for a work to lose its original intention. A century ago, pupils devoted themselves entirely to a teacher's style, which would be compatible with those of a choreographer, since the only schools in existence at that time were Italian, Russian, Danish, and French, each one with a specific style and way of working. Steps performed by any given dancer were so in tune with the way the body worked and with company traditions that the dancer probably could not move outside that sphere. As repertoires grew, dancers traveled more, companies hired more stars, things became more diversified, and ballet masters and dancers were no longer capable of retaining the nuances of ballets. The familiar works of the great composers would probably sound very different today if they had been handed down from one generation of musicians to the next with little or no written record of the composition. However thoughtfully music had been treated thereafter, under such circumstances it is unlikely that it would have remained very close to the original.

Dora Frankel described Benesh Notation, which looks similar to a music score, being written on a stave * and systemized in the same way. (See diagram.) Basically, it is as if the notator were behind the dancer plotting movement changes within a stave. Notation above the stave indicates rhythm and below it specifies the relationship of one dancer to another. Also, sometimes written between the staves is any point that will not fit on them, for example, extra information pertaining to contact.

---

* A set of five horizontal lines together with the corresponding four spaces between them, on which music is written.

An excerpt from the Benesh Movement Notation Score written by Dora Frankel of Glen Tetley's ballet Voluntaries.

There are only six symbols, and their placement and relativity determine position, with the body spanning the stave from head to foot. As legs normally work below the waist and arms above it, if there is a symbol with a light cross through it above what could be considered the waistline, it will be a leg, because it is an unusual place for it. The same applies to a sign with a light cross through it below the waistline, which indicates an arm position. Crosses denote an elbow or knee joint.

Peter Martins stated that one problem for contemporary choreographers and notators is that classical and modern steps are mixed and some of them lack names.

Referring to a ballet by Glen Tetley—*Pierrot Lunaire*—which is set to the powerful score by Arnold Schoenberg, involves three dancers and a soprano, and lasts thirty-seven minutes, Ms. Frankel said it would take approximately three months to do a master score, working exclusively on the ballet. A basic score is written in the rehearsal studio, but it is impossible to mark down all the information within rehearsal periods. The time spent taking notes in the studio is probably equaled by the hours given to cleaning up those notes. When a ballet is being created, it may take from three to six weeks to set. Then the master score must be completed, which entails inking and putting in the light cues. This takes a further six weeks. Most choreographers are working on so many ballets simultaneously that not much time can be devoted to any one. Ms. Frankel took four years to complete *Pierrot Lunaire*.

A choreographer does not simply dictate notes to a choreologist, because even though he may have worked out steps in advance he does not know precisely what he will do. The choreologist is part of the creative process and is present while the choreographer works his steps out with the dancers.

A competent choreologist can be indispensable to a choreographer, who sometimes needs assistance on working with the music. Problems can arise either if the choreographer cannot hear the music or if the pianist does not understand him. Having set certain steps, the choreographer may ask the choreologist to write them in canon,* so a choreologist must be a quick thinker and be prepared with an adequate supply of paper.

If a ballet already has been set without the choreologist's presence, he must work as fast as possible while a ballet is being rehearsed. Sometimes the choreography will be changed during this time, and the choreologist must make sure to make the appropriate notations.

* Consistent note-for-note imitation of one melodic line by another, in which the second line starts after the first.

Like Peter Martins, Dora Frankel dislikes working from a videotape, since she also feels it to be too imprecise. The tape displays individual dancers who may be off the music. As the picture is two-dimensional, the body cannot always be seen clearly. When the choreographer is creating, the choreologist can sense his intentions more accurately and be significantly more sensitive in notation. The sensitivity between the two artists is crucial, as dancers are quick to develop their own ideas. Should they misinterpret a choreographer's intentions, it will be necessary to refer back to the notation.

Sometimes a dancer may develop an idea offered to him by a choreographer that truly reflects the choreographer's intentions. When the great choreographers and dancers work together, there is usually a balance between what the choreographer indicates and what a dancer finally evolves. Ms. Frankel named the late John Cranko, director of the Stuttgart Ballet until his death in 1973, as a choreographer who would make suggestions to dancers that they would then transmute into movement. Anthony Dowell spoke of Sir Frederic Ashton, who would simply ask him to work out steps going from one particular spot to another. Ms. Frankel continued, "Many choreographers do that simply because their dancers are their instruments and they understand the qualities of any dancer they choose to work with. A choreographer wants to see how a dancer responds to little more than clues from him. Some, of course, have very specific ideas and just teach a dancer what they have worked out previously in their heads."

Many dancers have remarkable body memories, particularly of ballets that have been created on them. On occasion, a choreographer will ask a dancer who created one of his ballets to go through the work in order that the choreographer might be reminded of certain steps or nuances that have been lost. In 1967 Antony Tudor created *Shadowplay* for the Royal Ballet, with Anthony Dowell in the principal role, and later he set it on American Ballet Theatre. In the summer of 1979, while a member of that company, Anthony Dowell again danced in the role. "A couple of days after the first night, Tudor asked to see me, and I felt it was because I was not doing certain things the way he wanted them done. In fact, ABT had had *Shadowplay* in their rep for about a year and it had been taught from the Royal Ballet version and there were things that he just did not remember that I did. That ballet is always clear in my mind, but then, I remember most of the ballets that are created on me—such as *The Dream*, for example. I think it's mostly the secondhand ballets that I don't always remember when it comes to their being revived."

When a choreographer chooses to create a ballet on a particular dancer it is usually to employ the dancer's special attributes to the full. Since the dancer also helps in the creation, the work is normally so molded to his way of moving that he will remember the steps with as much facility as an actor would recall the lines of a role, written by a talented playwright, for which that actor was ideally suited.

Sometimes, having created a ballet on a dancer whom he considers ideal for the role, a choreographer will never again be able to find another dancer who captures the exact essence for which he is looking. "Even though a portrayal may be artistically valid in the opinion of the critics and the public," said Scott Barnard, "if it's not the vision the choreographer had, then his true intention will not come across."

Jean-Pierre Bonnefous, referring to the importance of a choreographer's musicality, cited George Balanchine. "Dancers have to work with many choreographers, some of whom have such an inadequate knowledge of music that their ballets don't relate to it. These are the ballets one has a hard time remembering. If dancers work with choreographers who are very musical, they understand increasingly more about music. The best ballets are the easiest to remember because they are the most logical, and you understand them so well that the steps come back. If they don't come back after you have been working with a choreographer for a while, then maybe the movements don't fit the music, or you didn't catch what the choreographer was saying or simply didn't understand."

Imagery is very important to dancers, and after a rehearsal of Antony Tudor's *Undertow* one of the corps members at American Ballet Theatre said she could not imagine trying to put together the ballet from notation, because Mr. Tudor *is* each character.

As he started that particular rehearsal, Mr. Tudor asked the dancers to sit on the floor so that he could check the casting for that night's performance. "You're not in it tonight; you're not; you wish you weren't!" He described to several how they should develop their characterization. Peter Fonseca was to dance the Transgressor, with whose emotional development the ballet is concerned. All the characters are from Greek mythology, and Mr. Tudor took each of the twenty-one in turn, including Aganippe, Nemesis, Medusa, Hymen, and the only muse—Polyhymnia. Although each character depicts its classical counterpart, the program notes say that "the names could be those of the inhabitants of any big city—for these characters can be found there." Mr. Tudor turned to one of the two Sileni. "Your walk is much too young. You're suffering from arthritis, rheumatism, and maybe carrying a balloon because you have no bladder and you're peeing into a bag, so use a little imagination." Moments later he turned to the pianist. "This is religious; it is vocal—not instrumental," a fact indicated by the inclusion of Polyhymnia in the cast. Each dancer's characterization was dealt with meticulously, and he told the company members of a dancer who once performed Hagar * in *Pillar of Fire* as if she were doing Cinderella, causing him constant frustration.

Scott Barnard spoke of Gerald Arpino. "Gerry's imagination is like a child's. He's never lost that quality, and he will push and push to try to get [what he wants]. The critics hit him sometimes for being distasteful, because he'll go beyond what classical ballet might call for to get the exuberance or whatever it is he's looking for on that particular occasion. But I think it would be fair to say that it is normal for a choreographer [that something will be lost in the process between what he sees in his mind's eye and what is actually depicted onstage]. I think the successful choreographer is the one who comes the closest to actually producing on the stage what he sees in his mind. It does not matter how imaginative a person is, if he can't produce his ideas onstage, a ballet won't work. I think that is why a choreographer is constantly changing little things within a ballet, no matter what its age, because he's still seeing a vision he hasn't quite captured."

Dancers are a choreographer's raw material, and as he creates on them, he is, to some extent, exposing his artistic capabilities extemporaneously. Even if he has specific steps in his head, a choreographer may not know exactly how they will look and may decide to make changes or adaptations according to the way a dancer manifests his idea. When creating a ballet there are many important points to be considered, and Jean-Pierre Bonnefous covered the basic procedure. "It is most important to have a clear idea in your head of what you want to project, or a ballet cannot work. It may take hours deciding how many people a piece is going to be choreographed for and how the movements are going to be divided for them. That is most important. The finale can't be half the ballet, for example, it has to be just at the end. In the case of a regular divertissement ballet, it should grow in numbers. You can't start the last movement with many dancers and finish with two. All those things are very important, and from there it is just a question of working with the dancers and trusting yourself enough to be in front of them.

"As a choreographer, I usually pick the music first, and I listen to it many times. Then I buy the score and if there are things I don't understand, I discuss them with a musician. For example, when I started to choreograph the Brandenburg Concerto No. 4 of Bach, I was rather unnerved because the music is so clear and I felt I should understand it better. The first movement needed light, happy choreography. The second movement had to be very simple, and the third move-

---

* Hagar, afraid that she has lost the love of her Friend to her Youngest Sister and fearing that she might become like her spinster Eldest Sister, gives herself to a dissolute young man, but later is reconciled with the Friend.

ment I found very hard to do. The first movement could not be choreographed too much on the ground and allowed little time for thought [when performing it], since it is allegro. It was important that the ballet was not too formal, nor the positions too exact. Space is very important for me. I want dancers to move a great deal, which is the Balanchine influence. Also, I try to adopt the freedom that is manifested in Paul Taylor's * ballets."

One way in which a choreographer may attempt to bring out the best in a dancer is by challenging him. Such challenges can sometimes make a dancer work in ways he finds particularly difficult, and may even make a dancer realize capabilities in himself he had previously been unable to recognize. Kay Mazzo talked of working with George Balanchine. "I've never been a good allegro dancer, and when I was a soloist Mr. Balanchine would give me steps that were extremely difficult for me to accomplish. His intention was to make me improve in a given area. I hated some of the things I had to do, but I told myself that it was important for me to try them. If a dancer continuously does easy steps there is not going to be any improvement."

Choreography serves as training for dancers, and Jean-Pierre Bonnefous emphasized the need for steps that give them a chance to improve, without being so contrary to the body's capabilities that they cause injuries. He does not believe that it is possible to become a good dancer without both good training and a demanding repertoire through which to learn. The dangers of an undemanding repertoire, he says, are that a dancer cannot improve. He then becomes stagnant and possibly will eventually lose interest in the dance.

The Balanchine style, which has been named neoclassical and is recognized as requiring many years of membership in the New York City Ballet in order that its intricacy and speed may be mastered, proved difficult even for Mikhail Baryshnikov during the fifteen months that he was a company member. Another Russian dancer, Alexander Godunov, used to dancing in the purely classical vein as a member of the Bolshoi Ballet until he left the Soviet Union in August 1979, found life in the West extremely demanding when he first arrived. When he first joined American Ballet Theatre, Mr. Godunov danced Balanchine's *Theme and Variations*. The ballet, contrary as it was to his usual style of working, made demands on his body to which he was totally unaccustomed. "As I was using muscles that I was not accustomed to working, I suffered from muscle fatigue. The only way to overcome such discomfort was by continuously working until I felt comfortable with the steps." Although he had expected his dancing life in the

* Paul Taylor is a modern-dance choreographer who has a dance company that bears his name.

West to be challenging, he had not expected his body to have to take quite such punishment.

Bart Cook remembers once dancing a piece for a choreographer who was totally unreasonable in his demands. Bart found the piece physically very difficult because it required being onstage for too long, having too much to do, and being surrounded by an excessive number of girls. Bart's sundry requests for some change in the choreography, or at least a moment when he might leave the stage, were repeatedly turned down, and he looks back on the experience as one of the most disastrous in his career. "Although I managed to get through the ballet, my blood must have been black from lack of oxygen. Balanchine does create hard steps, but at least he's open-minded, and when a dancer cannot do something he will change it. He is aware that it doesn't make that much difference. Once the feeling of a piece is set, a step changed here or there does not greatly alter a ballet. There are some novice choreographers who don't seem to appreciate that if the purpose of a ballet is not apparent, it won't work. Sometimes it's hard to recognize whether such choreographers have specific intentions or are just doing something to fill in space."

Merrill Ashley also spoke of the value of working with George Balanchine. "I remember once he did a variation for me which included a step that was extremely difficult, and I could only do it in practice clothes, not in costume. I worked on it and finally found a step based on what Mr. B. had done previously, and that I thought would work. When he saw the change I had made he allowed it, because he does not want to push a dancer into something that is really uncomfortable. Occasionally, he is emphatic about a certain movement and nothing else will do, but that happens infrequently. Mr. B.'s steps flow very naturally. If your body is going in one direction, the next step flows on from it; you don't have to fight. Many choreographers do a step, forget the momentum you have, and suddenly make you change direction. Consequently, there's a great deal of awkwardness to the movement. Balanchine is amazing to work with. It's as if he reaches into his pocket and comes out with some loose change—but his loose change comes in the forms of diamonds and pearls."

Robert Weiss became interested in choreographing very early in his dancing career, and for him it is the ultimate freedom. He reminds himself constantly of the importance of not making unreasonable demands on a dancer, because he feels a choreographer can become so absorbed with the image he has in mind that he has very little sympathy for any dancer. It is necessary to realize a dancer's limitations, which can be all too easily forgotten. Mr. Weiss has experienced dancing in one rehearsal, then attending a rehearsal as choreographer, and says that within five minutes of sitting at the second rehearsal, he has forgotten the difficulties of dancing. He finds it is easy to lose a sense of proportion, as so much more can happen mentally than physically.

There are choreographers who base their choreography on the level of expertise they see in class, which Dennis Nahat speaks very strongly against, saying that class is where one aims for the impossible, in order to be able to perform what can be reasonably demanded onstage.

In order for a choreographer to be able to teach his steps, he should be able to demonstrate them, as feeling the steps is one of the essences of good choreography. Jean-Pierre Bonnefous explained that a choreographer should be aware of approximately how long a step will take and that it is possible to make mental calculations only after many years of experience, as with George Balanchine. Since usually a choreographer does not know exactly how a dancer will move to a given piece of music, his timing cannot be precise. Steps that a choreographer thinks may take thirty seconds may take ten. One of the great advantages of being able to consult Mr. Balanchine, Mr. Bonnefous says, is that he has an acute sense of whether or not particular choreography will work. One drawback most male choreographers suffer is that they do not know the feeling of dancing on pointe. This lack of experience, Mr. Bonnefous feels, can be a real handicap when choreographing, as he says that doing the steps—pushing them in a certain direction—is actually how they come to mind, since dancers express themselves through their movements. There are several pointe work problems that can occur. For example, unlike a man, a woman cannot go on half pointe because she wears pointe shoes. Maybe a choreographer tries a step on half pointe and the woman finds it impossible. She needs to bend her knees and go onto pointe to start a movement, whereas a man can go straight onto half pointe. It is very hard, Mr. Bonnefous says, to keep that fact constantly in mind. He spoke of an occasion at the Paris Opera when Mr. Balanchine became concerned because the ballet master obviously was having difficulty demonstrating the choreographer's steps to the dancers. A ballet master must be able to show steps, and Mr. Bonnefous concluded, "If I try a step and I can't do it, I don't put it in a ballet, even if the dancers can do it, unless they look exceptionally good doing it. In that case, I ask them to teach it to me! If you listen to Balanchine, which is usually advisable, he says that a choreographer is principally a teacher, and that to choreograph you do not need only to have the ability to put steps together, you must be able to teach them. If you can do that, then you are a teacher."

Days before Peter Martins's ballet *Sonate di Scarlatti* was premiered by the New York City Ballet in Saratoga Springs, Mr. Martins worked with Bart Cook and

Peter Martins as choreographer during a New York City Ballet rehearsal.

New York City Ballet principals Heather Watts and Bart Cook in rehearsal with Peter Martins as they create his ballet Sonate di Scarlatti.

Heather Watts on the last few minutes of the pas de deux. They picked up from the last promenade, the point to which the ballet had been created, and the choreographer joked about wanting to steal a particular sequence of Balanchine steps that would have fitted the music ideally. He took Bart Cook's place and tried to establish whether Miss Watts could do a certain move up onto pointe. She reassured him she could if she was not pulled. Mr. Martins then replaced Heather Watts and, partnered by Bart Cook, maneuvered his 6-foot-2-inch frame through newly created steps to give himself a sense of what the ballerina would experience. Minutes later, after lighting a cigarette, Mr. Martins drank from a can of Pepsi, then asked the pianist to continue with Scarlatti's E Major Sonata. He stood motionless, eyes fixed to the floor, and listened.

They continued working on steps until Miss Watts announced she felt uncomfortable with a "hop, step, fouetté. I can't explain it, but if you did it, you'd see," she said. They straightened it out after a suggested change by Bart Cook, which Mr. Martins agreed to. Later on in the rehearsal Mr. Martins told Miss Watts that her arabesques should not be too swoopy. "This is straight out of Rossini," she responded. The choreographer walked through steps while the dancers sat for a moment. Miss Watts commented that "four piqués in a row don't look good." "I noticed," replied Mr. Martins. As the dancers started to work again, a smile came across his face. "Right now I know exactly what I want for the first time in this pas de deux."

Like most artists, choreographers develop a certain vocabulary that makes their works clearly identifiable. However, wondering whether or not he will be able to originate one that is strong enough to survive the years is the nightmare of every young dancer who considers becoming a choreographer. Trying to be original, Peter Martins believes, results in its antithesis. "I studied Balanchine's ballets intensely for at least five years. I practically photographed them in my mind, although I would not imitate them—but I wanted to use his idiom, his vocabulary, just as he used Petipa's. For example, I would register a ballet where he used angularities, a style I later chose for *Calcium Light Night*. Thank God that Balanchine has given us a vocabulary, because otherwise I don't think I could have choreographed. That sums it up. His ballets are a point of reference."

The reasons why a person is blessed with superior talent in any given field have never been established, and the general opinion is that talent is God-given. Robert Weiss talked of such inspiration. "I think Balanchine's style of working applies to any great artist, though I refer more to those who create than those who perform. Mr. Balanchine has said the idea is to become selfless at the moment of creation, in order to commune with God—or forces greater than oneself. I think that's true of anyone who has produced a superior work of art. If it's self-conscious, it fails. I think most outstanding artists would admit that, and those who wouldn't would be kidding themselves. Brahms said that no atheist could be a great composer, and I agree. Balanchine is a completely different person when he's choreographing an inspired work. I've seen him work on great ballets and he loses himself completely. He's almost in a trance. I don't mean to indicate that he loses consciousness, or that he's hypnotized, but he communes with a superior force and it flows out of him. He is an amazing craftsman, which is something that has to be learned, but to create a ballet of lasting worth, the craft and inspiration must come together. You should learn how to read a score and know the vocabulary of dance well enough to be able to put chains of steps together, but to make a ballet that's on the music with steps that flow is not simply a work of art. It's beyond that. Anyone who knows dance steps can put them together, but that doesn't make a ballet. Balanchine believes that man discovers; God creates. To be truly inspired takes that divine spark."

Of dancers, Ivan Nagy says, "Basically we're not creative. It's the choreographer who's the creative one. We are just little mailmen who deliver from the choreographer to the audience, although the degree of appeal that a performance has depends on the technical and artistic abilities of those who execute it."

5

Performances

*M*ost dancers live to perform. They are best able to express themselves when dancing, and for some it is the only aspect of life through which they feel fulfilled. Once they are onstage, cut off from the rest of the world, the harshness of reality cannnot harm them, for nothing exists for them beyond the curtain. Aware only of the other dancers onstage, in character roles they are relating to people who are as removed from reality at that moment as they are themselves. Living their fantasies together in a way that most people can only imagine, they escape within their characterization. In the abstract ballets, they concentrate totally on the technical demands. Following a good performance, they will float home. After a bad one, they may cry for two days.

The illusion does not end in the dancers' minds, for an effective performance carries the audience along with it. Apart from the general aura emanating from a particular ballet, its costumes, lighting, and scenery, each dancer also creates an optical illusion, and learns how to detract from either a malproportioned physique or specific technical weaknesses. For example, hips that are disproportionately wide, or big feet, can be deemphasized in the way a dancer moves or positions himself in relation to the audience. A large head can be counteracted, where possible, by a small headpiece, and vice versa.

The stage demands a great deal from performers, and gives small return to most, and riches and fame beyond the dreams of most to only a very few. The majority of company members are not dancing to become rich or famous, and are fully cognizant of the struggle it takes to survive the grueling daily life. There is probably no ballet dancer in the profession for the glamour. It is not glamorous to have to get up at ten with an aching body from the previous night, in order to rush to class at eleven and push that body through more hard work. It is not glamorous to be called in the event of an emergency and be given a few hours of rehearsal (if lucky) and then have to perform that night; or to be told after a day's traveling that a person who was supposed to be doing a particular part is indisposed and, without being mentally or physically prepared, having to appear onstage. It is even less glamorous having to keep up this pace for weeks, even months, on end, knowing an injury could take weeks to recover from, and the more tired the body as the season progresses, the greater the chance of that injury occurring.

As David Howard explained, "The stresses are tremendous, but it is through today's training and performing demands that dancers build their stamina. The competition is very intense, and for every dancer onstage there is a line of others waiting to take his place."

The direction a dancer's career takes depends not only on his own ability but also on the guidance he receives from his company director. David Howard has vivid memories of the incessant boredom he suffered while a corps member with the Royal Ballet. He remembers very little dancing.

In the classical ballets, not only is most of the dancing confined to the leads, but the demands on principals can seem almost unreasonable, such as the roles of Princess Aurora in *The Sleeping Beauty* and Albrecht in *Giselle*. During countless performances, Mr. Howard stood in the background as a "happy" or "unhappy" peasant, and depending on the occasion would dance either a polonaise or a waltz.

Many dancers are onstage because they were sent to class as young children and then coerced into working toward dance as a career. Larry Rhodes thinks this is probably true of the majority, and that it explains the unhappiness experienced by so many of them. Some dance only because of a fear of inadequacy in any other field—and fear, Mr. Rhodes believes, can produce great emotional dancing. He maintains that after many years the emotional life becomes centered around dance, becoming the only way dancers have of receiving their joys and rewards. When performing is the most important aspect of life, emotional development in other areas sometimes suffers, and day-to-day problems can become overwhelming.

Ballet involves every aspect of a dancer's being, and because its demands are so exacting, and most dancers have such high expectations of themselves, rarely do they leave the stage feeling satisfied after a performance.

Audience response does not touch a dancer if it is totally at variance with his own opinion of his performance. This is especially true if audience reaction is

Francis Sackett, New York City Ballet corps de ballet member, watches a performance from the wings.

New York City Ballet principals Sean Lavery and Merrill Ashley in George Balanchine's A Midsummer Night's Dream.

positive and the feelings of the dancers are negative. Whatever facade he may present, he will tend to stick with his own conclusions.

If there is anything more upsetting than a performance that is below par, it is an occasion when a dancer believes he is performing well, yet the audience is totally unresponsive. Said Ivan Nagy, "You feel you are dancing in front of stuffed cabbages and that everybody may as well go home."

The higher the level of a dancer's achievements, the higher his self-expectations. Upon retirement, Mr. Nagy claimed that there was not a single performance with which he had been totally happy. His retirement gala at the Metropolitan Opera House he found very uplifting, but technically "merely a question mark."

Natalia Makarova agrees that very rarely is she happy with a performance, but says that when she is, she feels very alive. "I equate performing with going to confession. You give of yourself, which is always satisfying. It is rare to be totally inspired, but it is important to be completely honest. If you superimpose a feeling that a role demands onto yourself, it comes across as somewhat false, and to avoid this you must identify with the character you are portraying. You have to have an image in which you believe completely the moment you go onstage, and you must be able to convince yourself. Emotions change with each performance. One moment I will decide to do a role with a certain feeling, and a few months later I am no longer comfortable with it because my inner state will have changed. It does not necessarily relate to how often you do a particular ballet, although it helps me to have fresh roles. I never tire of the classics, though, because I am constantly changing and finding something new to achieve."

A dancer must concentrate on many points during a performance, and except in cases where a ballet must be played directly to the audience to elicit response—such as with comedy—the presence of an audience is often a secondary factor. A performer may become so preoccupied with what he is doing that he can almost forget he is dancing for the benefit of others. He must consider the amount of space he has to work with, the kind of movement called for, technical requirements, and, where appropriate, the relationship involved in partnering and the portrayal of a character. Stage markings relative to choreography and light cues must be kept in mind, and with these combined factors requiring supreme coordination, he must ensure also that he dances with the music. Not only can an audience be almost unnoticed, but so can minor injuries. With the right mental approach, dancers have been known to overcome pain, and not until the moment of relaxation, when they have to walk in front of the curtain to take a bow, do problems come to the fore. Sometimes they suffer so badly they are hardly able to walk the few paces required. Occasionally they will collapse in the wings and find it impossible to return to the stage that day.*

As the appropriate mood is important for any performance, each dancer develops his own way of achieving the frame of mind befitting the character he will have to portray. For a classical ballet many will concentrate on a given day's performance from the moment they wake up in the morning. As Alexander Godunov said, dancers have to contend with the everyday problems that face most people and if they are depressed on the day of a performance of *Don Quixote* or extremely elated on a day they must dance *Giselle*, they have to use whatever method works best to change their frame of mind. As artists, their moods tend to be extreme. A dancer may feel that he has made a negative professional move that will go against him politically, and be morose and literally unapproachable for days. Then, upon discovering that he has been selected for a coveted role, he will suddenly be walking twelve feet above the earth—until the

---

* See Chapter 9, "Injuries and Physical Condition," page 145.

Merrill Ashley partnered by Sean Lavery in a New York City Ballet performance of The Four Temperaments *by George Balanchine.*

advent of another crisis. As a result of this, achieving an extreme change of mood requires total concentration, and many artists prefer to keep to themselves on performance days, except possibly to work privately with a favored teacher or ballet master for an hour or two on particular aspects of that day's performance.

Jimmy Dunne, a former member of the Harkness Ballet, the Joffrey Ballet, and Dancers, talked of the difficulty of giving the correct portrayal of a character when the technical requirements are also supremely demanding. The role of Albrecht in *Giselle* is a striking example. In Act I he woos the peasant girl Giselle, despite being already engaged to another, and upon discovering his falsehood, Giselle goes mad and dies. Consequently, in Act II the Queen of the Wilis * orders Albrecht to dance to his death. The man's choreography is exhausting, yet all the time he is dancing the second act Albrecht must appear to be a contrite, repentant character pleading for his life.

The dancer, who wants nothing more than to be able to stop and catch his

* According to Slavic and German legends, the spirits of betrothed girls who have died as a result of being jilted.

breath, must keep up his frantic pace of dancing, portray the sensitivity of his character, and make it appear the most natural of achievements. As Mr. Dunne explained, "All the physical elements of your body are involved, which changes your psyche. If you stay onstage after dancing very hard, usually your whole body throbs because your blood is rushing so hard. The muscles are exhausted, and I think many people mistake that feeling for pain."

As a dancer's entire being is involved in a performance, when it is time to leave the theatre, rarely will he go home and sleep. Usually this is the time for the main meal of the day, and his mood will determine whether he eats at home in front of the television or with a group of friends in a restaurant. If the performance has gone well and he is in high spirits, it will possibly be the latter. If he is slightly melancholic, or if some part of his body feels strained, he may prefer to be by himself, or at most to share the events that have just happened with someone to whom he feels close. Frequently, it will be the time for lying on the sofa with ice packs on sore, aching feet. Given the opportunity, a dancer will probably spend the rest of the evening talking about the performance, or at least thinking about it. If watching Johnny Carson, he will probably be aware of little more than the images on the screen.

Mikhail Baryshnikov, together with New York City Ballet corps de ballet boys, in Prodigal Son *by George Balanchine.*

A New York City Ballet performance of Interplay *by Jerome Robbins. Left to right: Douglas Hay, Peter Frame, Timothy Fox, and Christopher Fleming.*

What dancers gain from performing varies with each individual. For Ivan Nagy, "It's a question I've never been able to answer—and it's not due to the language barrier, because I can't even do it in Hungarian! There is a commitment, a love; one's imagination is fed with a fantastic feeling."

In an age where very little is left to the imagination, even ballet and opera have resorted to exhibitionism on occasion, determined not to be outdone by more popular forms of entertainment. Mr. Nagy dislikes seeing any form of entertainment sensationalized, believing that it is far more vitalizing to feed the imagination by awakening the senses rather than bombarding them. "In ballet, especially, I think we are able to give a feeling for eroticism and nudity without actually displaying it. Earthiness I think is gorgeous, I'm no prude, but vulgarity I can't take. Onstage it is so cheap, and there is a fine line between what is earthy and what is vulgar."

The amount of time a dancer takes to prepare himself before a performance depends on many factors: how many hours he has spent in rehearsal that day; the type and length of ballet; whether he is new to or experienced in the role; and also, to some extent, his age. If he has spent most of the day in the studios, then a

Jean-Pierre Frohlich of the New York City Ballet dances the role of Puck in Jerome Robbins's ballet The Four Seasons.

dancer in his teens or twenties may spend only twenty to thirty minutes warming up before a performance. A role in a classical ballet will require that the body is properly warmed up to avoid injury, as will participation in any strenuous ballet. *Etudes*, by Harald Lander, displays the technique of classical ballet from the simplest to the virtuoso steps. It requires great stamina and, because it shows classroom technique, must be executed with maximum expertise. Consequently, a dancer must go onstage as well prepared as possible.

Cynthia Gregory, Anthony Dowell, and Adam Lüders say they probably spend thirty to forty minutes at the barre before appearing onstage. Total preparation usually takes one to two hours, but a young dancer facing a first major role will frequently take longer. If rehearsals are at the theatre, he may not leave from the time he arrives to start work that day. Sitting in his dressing room at the Metropolitan Opera House, Anthony Dowell described his routine. "I arrive two hours before a performance and warm up in the dressing room because it's such a long traipse to the stage. I have enough room in here," he said, referring to the spaciousness and comfort of the large room, complete with shower. "I enjoy the privacy, rather than the distraction of being on the stage. A few minutes ahead of

Martine van Hamel, American Ballet
Theatre principal, in Harald Lander's
Etudes.

Former New York City Ballet principal
Jean-Pierre Bonnefous with corps de ballet
member Linda Homek in a performance of
The Four Temperaments,
choreographed by George Balanchine.

time I will go and try things out." As a dancer's perspective changes with experience, so does the way he works. "In my youth, my nerves were devoted mainly to physical energy. I think we all have our crosses to bear with regard to our nerves, and my problem has always been wondering whether I have the strength to get through a performance. At one time, when I started to work at the barre, my nerves used to make me so weak that I realized I was wasting energy, so I would simply limber up and run around. Now, though, I have to take out more of an insurance policy on the body. I feel I have to go through the basic exercises, although I have a hard time making myself do it."

Corps members can be at a disadvantage when preparing for a performance, as they must share their dressing rooms, sometimes with many others. Some will be working their way toward a lighthearted ballet, while others will need to develop a serious frame of mind. Christian Holder, a former member of the Joffrey Ballet (and nephew of Geoffrey Holder), regards ballets in a very personal way. "I like to think of them as people. It's like knowing how to relate to a friend. If you know how to talk to them and make them happy, it helps. I know that acting a certain way will bring out the best in people, and I try to treat ballets accordingly."

Greg Huffman rests for about fifteen minutes upon arrival at the theatre. If he feels low while putting on his makeup, he looks at himself in the mirror and makes faces. This, he finds, can elevate his mood and bring him into a character. "Your sense of self leaves you and you become somebody else. The illusion takes over, which is very important."

While performing, it is necessary for a dancer to keep moving constantly, because the muscles are being tuned and the blood must be kept flowing. During a strenuous role a dancer does not disappear into the wings and sit down to await his next entrance, because then it is a shock to the system when he continues. Unfortunately, the way some of the classical ballets are staged in relation to the choreography is not conducive to warm muscles. In the black act of *Swan Lake*, in the American Ballet Theatre staging, after entering with his mother, Prince Siegfried takes his place beside her on one of the two thrones at the side of the stage. The setting is that of a grand ball during which the Prince is expected to select a bride from among the six princesses who are presented to him, and the Prince and his mother watch the character dances. As the dancer sits on the throne, not only are his muscles cooling, but he may also become nervous before going into what is technically the most difficult pas de deux in the ballet. This he must dance with the Black Swan, Odile, who appears in the guise of Odette, with whom the Prince has fallen in love. When she enters with the evil magician, Rothbart, they present themselves as the Baron von Rothbart and his daughter. The Baron has

New York City Ballet principals Bart Cook and Karin von Aroldingen in Violin Concerto, *choreographed by George Balanchine.*

New York City Ballet corps de ballet members in Le Tombeau de Couperin, *choreographed by George Balanchine.*

cast a spell over Odette and other princesses, turning them into swans. Only at night do they appear in their human form. Should a man prove faithful in his love for Odette, the magician's spell will be broken. By appearing at the ball, Rothbart hopes to coerce the Prince into committing himself in marriage to Odile, thus betraying Odette. The black act pas de deux is one that no man takes lightly, and Anthony Dowell elaborated. "In the Ballet Theatre production I sit on that throne and go straight into the pas de deux, whereas in the London [Royal Ballet] production I meet Odile and we go offstage before the character dances start, so I'm in the wings being able to keep warm. Production-wise it doesn't look so good. It makes much more sense if the Prince watches the dances, but I get bored and restless, which is why I get up and move around [the stage in the American production]. I just couldn't sit there. It's dreadful because you know you're not properly warm."

In the productions of the Bolshoi Ballet and the Ballet Nacional de Cuba the Prince leaves the stage. Rudolf Nureyev departs into the wings when dancing with American Ballet Theatre. The Prince needs an audience's sympathy, as not only is he faced with the imminent approach of the pas de deux, but his nerves are not helped by his knowledge that he must keep his body warm.

Cynthia Gregory spoke of the way she prepared to go onstage. "I usually start thinking about a role as I'm putting my makeup on. I decide how the makeup

should look, then once the costume is on, I have developed a sense of the character. I'm never really intense in the wings, I'm the type who can laugh and joke
and then go on expressing a totally different mood. I prefer to forget my role for a
second and then go on fresh." Most dancers initially put on their makeup and do
their hair, then put on the costume, and finally warm up until the time comes to
appear onstage. Girls sometimes choose this time to clean their pointe shoes.

Makeup is a very important aspect of characterization, and the better the
dancer's sense of his role, the better his makeup will probably be. Fine points of
makeup and costume are an extension of a performance and are all part of the
way a dancer expresses himself. Robert Joffrey is known to be a stickler for
neatness, and before a performance he will be seen backstage with a can of hair
spray, eliminating any stray wisps of hair that dancers have. It is difficult to keep
hair neatly arranged while performing, and as a precautionary measure many will
dab on Elmer's Glue-All.

*Corps de ballet member Douglas Hay being made up for a performance with the New
York City Ballet.*

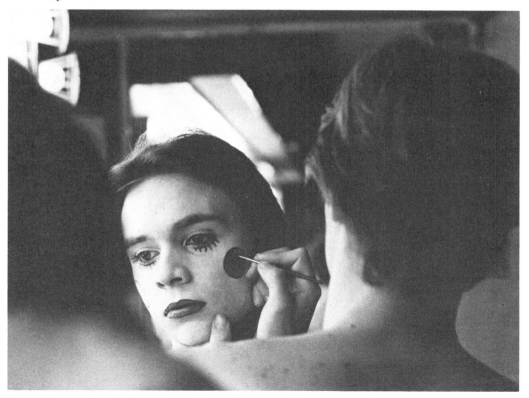

Maria Calegari, New York City Ballet soloist, securing her headpiece before a performance of George Balanchine's Swan Lake.

Elise Flagg, while a corps de ballet member with the New York City Ballet, preparing for a performance.

In the process of warming up before a performance a dancer has to be careful not to work so hard that he is left without enough stamina to finish the performance, which is a trap that inexperienced dancers can fall into.

To design dance costumes requires unique expertise, for they must have the right look and be practical to move in. Anthony Dowell, who designs costumes, spoke of the advantages of being a dancer-designer. "One knows what one wants! Most of the time you rehearse in practice clothes, and suddenly you are in the first rehearsal where you use the costumes, and when you try to move, it's as if you were trapped. To design a formal doublet for a classical ballet which doesn't gape at the neck when you lift your arms is terribly hard. It must appear to have some substance and yet fit like a second skin. One of the best costumes I've ever worn was designed by Santo Loquasto for *Other Dances.** It's not just that the design is attractive, it is that in the workroom they found a way to make it look as if it were three separate pieces—tights, shirt, and waistcoat. In fact, it is all one piece and I step into it. It's made of spandex, and when I move the costume stretches instead of riding up, so it stays perfectly in place. I've learned something from that. It would be wonderful if one's classical costumes could be made in that way. Cleaning those is difficult and expensive because of the embroidery and jewelry, whereas the spandex costume goes into a washing machine." Another disadvantage to embroidered costumes is that dancers can become hooked together when dancing a pas de deux. Often they manage to unhitch themselves gracefully in such a way that the audience never notices. Sometimes they are not so fortunate, and Anthony Dowell remembers such occa-

* Pas de deux choreographed by Jerome Robbins to music of Chopin and created by Natalia Makarova and Mikhail Baryshnikov.

Karin von Aroldingen in George Balanchine's A Midsummer Night's Dream *at the New York City Ballet. Sean Lavery looks on.*

sions. "Once when Antoinette [Sibley] and I were in Australia, she got the knicker legs of her tutu caught on the hook of my costume during a performance of *Cinderella* and we couldn't unhitch, so I had to run off with her. Then it happened again with Natasha [Natalia Makarova] in Los Angeles when we were performing *Don Q*. [*Quixote*]. The stage manager said afterward that he had been tempted to come on with a bucket of water and pour it over us because we reminded him of a pair of dogs! Fortunately, in a ballet like *Don Q*. you can treat it for laughs, which we did, and it went fine. If it happened in *Swan Lake* it would be disastrous!"

Jimmy Dunne has also experienced some hazardous moments relating to costume. "While a member of the Harkness Ballet I once had to appear in a costume that was so heavy it was restricting. Luckily, we didn't have to dance as it was just for the procession at the end of *Firebird*. We were all dressed as icons, each one in a different full-length costume, which looked exquisite. The trouble was that they were extremely heavy and we were much too hot. The fifteen of us onstage kept colliding, which didn't really suit the atmosphere too well. Another time, I had to do an Indian dance wearing a very uncomfortable headdress, and the variation was impossible. The choreographer had studied the ritual dances of the Hopi

Mikhail Baryshnikov in George Balanchine's Apollo *with the New York City Ballet.*

Sean Lavery partners Merrill Ashley at the New York City Ballet in Jerome Robbins's ballet In G Major.

Indians in Oklahoma, and when we went there to perform they were invited. He found out that their goddess was a spider, and the dance depicted a spider woman coming down from the rafters on a swing and Indians jumping around her and dancing with her. The Indians got up during the performance and marched out of the theatre because we had bastardized their religion. For that reason, we didn't do it again. My headdress made it impossible for me to do the choreography and I fell down about four times. There was a veil attached to the mask I was wearing, which they omitted to tell me they had painted right before the curtain went up, because the choreographer had decided he wanted a little more color! When veil is painted you can't see through it, so in the middle of the performance I had to rip it off. It was a nightmare.''

Quick costume changes are frequently necessary during a performance, and usually a dresser will be waiting in the wings to help. Jimmy Dunne recalls one of the quickest changes he has ever made, which he estimated took about twenty seconds. "I had to put on a jump suit that had one zipper, and as I had people there to help me, I just jumped into it and ran out. Such fast changes are very difficult, especially as you are perspiring. There is plenty of baby powder involved, and you pull on a tight-fitting costume amidst a cloud of white dust."

The degree of hardness in a pair of pointe shoes varies according to the ballet in which a dancer is performing. Natalia Makarova explained some of the differences. "*Giselle* is a romantic ballet with a light and airy quality, and Giselle herself is always above the ground. When I dance, it irritates me enormously if I can hear myself, because noise destroys the performance, so I prefer to dance on my toes." Even though it seems as if this would be extremely painful, Miss Makarova laughed and claimed that she is used to it. "*Swan Lake* is a little different because it doesn't require that airy quality. It contains more technical steps, like pirouettes, for example, that need stronger, supporting shoes." In this ballet the Swan Queen normally wears out a pair of shoes in each act. Miss Makarova says she wears softer shoes in the white act (where the Prince and Odette first meet beside the lake and fall in love) than in the black act. In the latter, there are thirty-two fouettés in the coda, for which the standing foot must be given adequate support.

Corps members, as well as the ballerina, need fairly soft pointes to their shoes when performing in certain ballets. This applies in the two white acts of *Swan Lake*, for example, and before a performance ritualistic banging is sometimes to be heard backstage as the girls knock the hardness out of their pointe shoes. Kay Mazzo describes the procedure in the dressing rooms at the New York State Theater as sounding like the "Anvil Chorus."

Most members of an audience have little or no knowledge of the process involved in staging a performance. They will notice an obvious technical error such as a wandering spotlight, but the majority of minor slips will go unnoticed. Live performances mean excitement to an audience, while for the stage manager they are times when he has to be constantly on the alert, not only following previously set cues but watching for any last-minute changes that may have been made without his having been notified.

When a company the size of American Ballet Theatre dances at the Metropolitan Opera House, the crew working under the stage manager never consists of fewer than twenty men, often involves about twenty-seven, and for certain very complicated productions, such as ballets of several acts, can require even more. Not only must the timing be split-second, but as heavy sets are rolled on and off the stage, and lowered and raised from above it, there is always the risk of accident. The stage manager asks the dancers to leave the stage during an intermission, but there is occasionally one who will delay to test a certain step he is not happy with or another who will return before the stage manager announces over the intercom to the dancers in the dressing rooms that it is time to come back to the stage. "They don't seem to realize the dangers," said Jerry Rice. "Once when we were in Washington, in the middle of a scene change that was going very badly, part of a set came down from overhead like a spear to the floor. A propman was walking by, and I would estimate that it fell not more than six inches in front of him. Had it struck him it would have gone right through his head. For a couple of days after that I was successful in keeping the dancers offstage during intermissions, but then they started to forget and drift back again."

Jimmy Dunne described intermissions from the dancers' point of view. "Dancers want to keep moving to keep the blood circulating, and when you're in a

Heather Watts and Mikhail Baryshnikov in George Balanchine's Orpheus *with the New York City Ballet.*

Peter Martins performs the title role in Orpheus.

Peter Martins with other New York City Ballet members in George Balanchine's Orpheus.

small theatre it can become especially confusing. It is very active usually, with stagehands, lighting and costume designers, and choreographers. I think it can be very difficult for stagehands. They may try to move a set and a dancer happens to be standing in the way, oblivious that a set is coming in his direction. Then comes the cry 'heads up.' When you hear that you stop what you're doing and move very fast, because you realize if you don't you're going to get hurt."

The stage manager has to adapt to the dancers with whom he is working. Some need more notice than others when they are called to return to the stage. "I've always had to wait for Natasha [Natalia Makarova] and Gelsey [Kirkland], so I try to compensate by putting out the calls early," said Mr. Rice. "Unfortunately, though, I think they eventually figured out what was going on! In cases like that I usually call their dressing rooms to make sure they will be ready before the audience is alerted to return to the auditorium." If a dancer has to completely redo her hair and makeup between ballets, she will usually approach the stage manager before leaving the stage and ask him to stretch the intermission slightly. She may even ask to be excused from taking a bow at the end of her first ballet to give her extra time to prepare for the next one.

Bows and curtain calls are considered as much a part of the performance as ballet itself. They are organized so that each dancer enters as instructed, and only injury or prior permission permits him to leave the stage without appearing. If one dancer is missing in a line, it may have to be restaged, as it will be off balance. A partner may even stand waiting for the other to appear and find himself standing alone feeling slightly foolish. The Ballet Nacional de Cuba choreographs curtain calls in character, so that as a dancer appears through the

New York City Ballet corps de ballet girls in George Balanchine's Symphony in Three Movements.

Patrick Bissell, American Ballet Theatre principal, in Glen Tetley's Contredances.

curtain he will leap into the air or give some other flourish that fits the occasion.

It is the ballet master's job to inform the stage manager before a performance if a change has been made. This may occur in casting, which the stage manager must announce to the audience over the microphone before the curtain goes up. A dancer may be suffering a slight injury or be stepping into a role at the last minute, which means a variation may have been cut out to reduce the load on him. Mr. Rice says that, unfortunately, very often a ballet master forgets to inform the stage manager of any changes, and most frequently it is the dancers who will let him know of them.

Though they occur infrequently, inevitably mistakes happen that blot an otherwise smooth performance. Jerry Rice acknowledged he has had his share of catastrophes. "The worst time, I think, was during the premiere of Baryshnikov's staging of *Nutcracker*. During the first act, one mistake happened and it became compounded. It was an absolute disaster. Mischa was absolutely livid, as well he should have been. I apologized to him during the intermission, repeatedly telling him how sorry I was. 'Public does not know sorry,' came the reply, and he is right. The public does not come to see mistakes, and any they do see, I believe, are the fault of the stage manager. Whether the problem can be solved or not is not an issue. It's still my responsibility. With that attitude, I'm surprised I don't have an ulcer, because there are things that are beyond my control. Unfortunately, I don't like to believe that's possible. You like to think you have total control, and it's not true!"

Talking onstage during a performance is not uncommon because, as Greg Huffman said, "Dance is a feeling; it's not just jumping through the air. Saying something or just letting out a sound can help give you the feeling for the impetus you need."

Jerome Robbins has choreographed a comic masterpiece called *The Concert*. While listening to a pianist playing music of Chopin, the characters in the ballet dance their fantasies. The cast includes a married couple with no love lost between them, and the husband makes one entrance dressed as a cossack. He leaps from the wings and emits a loud roar. Henpecked by his wife, for a few minutes the husband imagines himself as a fearless man with total control over her. Jean-Pierre Bonnefous, who danced the role at the New York City Ballet, said that the roar is a marvelous way of giving the feeling needed to the dancer playing the character.

During a performance of *Swan Lake*, Anthony Dowell came offstage into the wings near the end of the black act to follow the disappearing Odile, whom he has at that point decided to marry. "Oh, please," he said in the wings as he took his partner, Natalia Makarova, by the hand to lead her back onstage. "My talking is used as a way of making myself relax," he said afterward. "It has nothing to do with the person I'm with. Sometimes I suppose the audience must be able to hear it. It depends on a theatre's acoustics and what kind of music is playing." In a performance of *Don Quixote* he called encouragement to Yoko Ichino dancing the role of Kitri, as she was going through the very demanding third-act variation.

Talking is used also to express frustration or release tension, and under such circumstances swearing onstage is not uncommon. It is all part of the poetry.

Hugo Fiorato is the associate conductor at the New York City Ballet, but he sometimes conducts for other companies. Where there is weak artistic direction, he says, often a dancer decides the tempo of a piece of music to which he is performing. "What they sometimes don't realize is that it is to their own detriment to destroy the tempo, because then the music has no life or swing and then they don't feel like dancing. Sometimes a knowledgeable choreographer may ask the conductor to slow down the tempo just a hair—and that is exactly what they mean. That can make such an enormous difference to dancers and it won't destroy the music. There are certain ballets at City Ballet that are perennial problems. Some of the Bournonville choreography we use involves such tradition, which usually means bad taste. It's been through so many hands and each individual has thrown in his two cents' worth. As a result, you spend the entire ballet jumping from one tempo to another."

Inevitably in the course of Mr. Fiorato's traveling around the world with the New York City Ballet, unfortunate situations have arisen in performances that have made them memorable. He recalls an occasion in Bologna, Italy, that happened about twenty-five years ago. "I was supposed to prepare eight ballets, and the orchestra had been recruited from local restaurants. They could hardly read any music at all, and after listening to a rehearsal Balanchine told me in his thick Russian accent that I should take a machine gun and shoot them all! He wanted to cancel, but the management was upset because the house was sold out, so we

Cynthia Gregory and Ivan Nagy of American Ballet Theatre in a performance of Concerto *choreographed by Kenneth MacMillan.*

Patrick Bissell, principal, and Lise Houlton, soloist, with American Ballet Theatre corps members in Glen Tetley's Contredances.

Karin von Aroldingen, Kipling Houston, and Maria Calegari of the New York City Ballet dance George Balanchine's Serenade.

chose two of the easiest pieces—*Serenade** and Benjamin Britten's *Young People's Guide to the Orchestra*. When it came to the performance of *Serenade* we just got through the first movement and into the second movement, which contains a lovely waltz. There is a section where the first violins play a melody and the second violins repeat it, and the two sections go back and forth. We proceeded, and one by one they all dropped out until not a soul was playing. The dancers had to keep going, so I sang the music, and in the same manner in which they had faded out, the violinists all came in again, although by that time the dancers onstage were shaking with laughter. Another time we had a dear, elderly Italian harpist in an orchestra, who had to play the *Young People's Guide to the Orchestra*. She had gray hair, and she leaned forward to look at the script and then looked up at me and said, '*Maestro, non posso; non posso!*' ['I can't; I can't!'] I told her not to worry, that she should study it and then I would go over it with her. She improved with each rehearsal, and finally came the day of the performance. She sat there going *frrm, frrm, frrm,* and getting progressively slower. Finally I couldn't stay with her because the ballet was suffering, so I went right on past her. We got through her variation and at the end she was still playing. To this day, occasion-

---

* To the music of Tchaikovsky's Serenade for String Orchestra in C Major, with the third and fourth movements transposed.

Gelsey Kirkland as the Sylphide in La Sylphide *with American Ballet Theatre.*

ally when there is a hectic moment on stage, Mr. B. will look at me and say, '*Maestro, non posso; non posso.*' ''

For a dancer to acquire proficient technique is an outstanding accomplishment, but to acquire proficient technique in partnering is the ultimate. Both dancers need to be cooperative. The man must be able to lift his partner smoothly, have a good sense of her balance, and learn to understand the areas in which she needs help. Such exacting demands are hard to realize, as Martine van Hamel has learned. ''I think it's more difficult finding the ideal partner than the ideal husband! Not that it's easy to find either, but there are so few male dancers.''

Peter Martins and Suzanne Farrell have long been acclaimed as a perfect partnership, but Mr. Martins disagrees with the general opinion of what that entails. "Most people feel that partnering is ninety percent physical, but that it requires a special rapport which they claim Suzanne and I have. I think that is nonsense. It may be true of some partnerships, but certainly not ours. We have no rapport. We never speak to each other offstage. Our rapport is purely physical. Our bodies move in the same way. She's tall, and when I see her attack a certain step I

Gelsey Kirkland performs the role of the Sylphide with American Ballet Theatre corps members in a performance of La Sylphide.

Martine van Hamel and Michael Owen perform with American Ballet Theatre in Etudes *by Harald Lander.*

can identify with her. I know what she's going to do because, being tall myself, I would do the same thing."

Several ballet partnerships are considered legendary, including that of Dame Alicia Markova and Anton Dolin. While speaking of his own great partnership one afternoon in London, Mr. Dolin mentioned others: Pavlova and Mordkin; Karsavina and Nijinsky; Fonteyn and Nureyev; Wright and Gilpin; Sibley and Dowell; and, currently, Makarova and Dowell. To those should be added Alonso

Above and below, Marianna Tcherkassky and Fernando Bujones, American Ballet Theatre principals, in the pas de deux from Rendezvous *by Steffan Jan Hoff.*

and Youskevitch; Fracci and Bruhn; and Kirkland and Baryshnikov.

Later, in New York, Natalia Makarova commented on her partnership with Anthony Dowell. "I love to dance with Anthony. I always feel secure in his arms because he is strong, yet also gentle. He's a very sensitive person, and I think we have a very nice mutual response. We're not working against each other," she added, laughing.

Anthony Dowell is the only dancer to have been involved in two illustrious partnerships. Mr. Dowell feels, "My partnership with Natasha is wonderful and I'm very happy with it, but even in my days partnering Antoinette I always realized the necessity of dancing with different partners. You need that to regenerate an ongoing partnership. . . . Antoinette and I danced in unison. We looked good together, had the same musicality, and got on well in our work. I

At the New York City Ballet, George Balanchine's Tzigane *is performed by Suzanne Farrell and Peter Martins.*

New York City Ballet principal Patricia McBride in Coppelia.

think a harmonious relationship is essential because the life is so strenuous."

As outstanding technique becomes more and more prevalent in companies, and many fear that artistry is on the decline, Yoko Ichino commented on some young male dancers: "Nowadays they are so busy training young boys to do phenomenal tricks, they forget to teach them the art of partnering." Cynthia Gregory believes that boys must learn, if only the hard way, because a man who is not good at partnering will not look good himself. "Many contemporary ballets require very intricate partnering, and to carry them off well a man must be competent. I think the boys coming up now are starting to realize that partnering is a very important part of performing. I don't think partnering should be competitive. I can't compete with a man's jumps and double tours, and he can't compete with my pointe work and delicacy. Of course, part of the excitement in a bravura pas de deux is seeing who will outdo who [in the variations]."

Partnering requires great strength on the part of the man, and if a woman is not easy to lift, as Anthony Dowell said, "You can have the feeling of being a forklift!'' Although the woman's weight and height in proportion to the man are a consideration, there are some tall women who are considered easy to partner because they aid a man by pushing off the floor at the precise moment of the lift, in order to help with the elevation. Cynthia Gregory and Karin von Aroldingen (a principal with the New York City Ballet) are two such dancers. Just because a woman is petite does not automatically mean she will be easy to lift. If she does not know how to help her partner at the crucial moment, as one man said from experience, ''She can be ninety-five pounds of solid lead!''

Cynthia Gregory is partnered frequently by Rudolf Nureyev. She says she is just under six feet when on pointe, making her slightly taller than he. With the expertise they have developed in working together, the difference in their height becomes secondary. Miss Gregory spoke affectionately of their partnership. ''He's not really tall enough for me, but he's so determined that he makes things work. It's a very secure feeling knowing you're with a partner who is not going to give up. He'll just look you in the eye, lead or follow, and generally work with you. I think all of the young principals in the company [American Ballet Theatre] have learned from watching him.''

Nina Fedorova, corps member, and principal Robert Weiss as Titania and Oberon in George Balanchine's A Midsummer Night's Dream *with the New York City Ballet.*

Mikhail Baryshnikov in Jerome Robbins's Afternoon of a Faun *with the New York City Ballet.*

Many of the steps and poses in partnering appear dangerous to the audience, and certainly very precarious for the girl, yet Martine van Hamel said of those moments, "By the time you appear onstage usually you have all the intricacies worked out. Lifts are not necessarily the most dangerous aspect of partnering. You rarely fall on your head. The only thing that could happen is that something could look ugly. Some turns can be very precarious, although they don't appear that way, and vice versa."

Ballet, Ivan Nagy believes, "is the original women's lib profession. That is very important to remember in classical ballet. When the curtain goes up you have to follow her rhythm, even if it does not fit the music's phrasing. The critics refer to that as 'interestingly phrased.' It's unmusical, in my opinion, but you cannot let her know that. If you follow her, it plays down the fact that she is wrong, and then the audience thinks the incorrect phrasing is intentional."

There are seven movements in dancing: élancer, to dart; étendre, to stretch; glisser, to slide; plier, to bend; relever, to raise, to lift; sauter, to jump; and tourner, to turn. All steps in dance are based on one or more of these actions simultaneously. For example, a double tour en l'air (double turn in the air) involves both jumping and turning.

To some extent, a dancer's technique usually will develop in a manner appropriate to his build, and when he becomes aware of his strong points he will concentrate on them. He may be better at jumping than turning, or strong in adagio rather than allegro choreography.

Adam Lüders with girls from the corps de ballet of the New York City Ballet in George Balanchine's The Four Temperaments.

Until recently, a dancer who was a true artist was able to compensate some-what for inadequate technical capabilities. This is no longer the case. As technical standards go higher each year, companies easily are able to find well-trained young people hoping for a chance to work. From the many who are eligible, directors look for those whom they consider to be expressive and have artistic potential.

Usually, men are better at jumping than women, because in training, during the time the girls are studying pointe work, boys are able to concentrate on their jumps and turns. Certain skilled dancers have a light, airy quality in the way they spring from the floor, remain suspended in the air at the height of the jump, and land softly, only to spring off the floor again. The technique is known as ballon, as in the bouncing of a ball. The great male dancer Vaslav Nijinsky was said to have had astonishing ballon, like few others since.* Fernando Bujones spoke of the technique involved in staying suspended in the air. "It's timing and coordina-tion of the body. Even the breathing has to have a certain timing. You have to feel that your whole body freezes for a second without your even blinking. That gives the illusion of staying in the air. Of course, to do that you have to have the natural ability." It is also necessary to be well trained.

Ballet movement is based on physics, and as a racing driver alters his car to cut vital seconds from his lap time, so a dancer develops subtle ways of refining his movement so that he uses minimum energy to maximum effect. A girl will take a different approach to a step depending on whether she is dancing on pointe or demi-pointe. On pointe she turns faster because she is dancing on a smaller surface and there is less friction. However, on pointe there is also less traction and push. To go up onto pointe requires a different force from going up onto demi-pointe. For the former, she must go fast because she has farther to go and if she does not put sufficient energy into the move she will not manage. Depending on the steps being danced, being on pointe can be harder because of the small surface on which the girl is standing, but sometimes it can be easier because the balance is finer.

The auditorium in which a dancer has to appear can profoundly affect his performance, as Jimmy Dunne explained. "You're not necessarily aware of the people. There is a void—a dark feeling. You're blinded by lights and all you can see are the exit signs and a black mass out there. It's a mysterious feeling, and when you're performing your mind does change, your sensitivity is different, even your balance. When you're using footlights they drown out everything, but without them you can see the front rows of the audience. That fact causes you to

---

* A member of Diaghilev's Ballet Russe, Nijinsky stopped dancing in 1917.

relate to them differently, I think. Also, you relate to an audience differently than you would to observers in a studio, since the opinions of the latter often have far more crucial consequences. However, an audience can be a magnet that pulls you. Sometimes in performance I've achieved technical feats that I've never been able to do in class, because of the lightness I have felt onstage." Peter Martins said of audiences, "I am a performer and I take the stage in my hands, but the thought of three thousand pairs of eyes watching me makes me rather uncomfortable."

Live theatre, not surprisingly, has a rich history of performances that are remembered more for the misadventure that befell them than for the events themselves, and dancers have suffered many such experiences.

Ivan Nagy has a vivid memory for such moments. "The worst disaster I ever had happened on an opening night at the State Theater [with American Ballet Theatre]. I was doing *Baiser de la Fée* with Cynthia [Gregory], and it is a murderous ballet because you have to do it on counts. It's also very awkward because the girl's skirt has so many layers. At one point, instead of catching her, I just got the skirt with my thumb, and she slid down until she was so close to the floor that the only thing between her and disaster was my thumb. If I had tried to change hands she would have kissed the floor, and obviously I didn't want that. I knew instinctively there was no way to pick her up gracefully, and thought the only way was to take a run. So I charged to the first wing, pushing a little bit. Eventually, when I picked her up I looked at Cynthia and asked her where we were. She had no idea. The pas de deux continued to be unrecognizable as we failed to pick up again on the choreography before the end. It was worse than going to the dentist. We just kept flowing and running, and at one point Cynthia said she knew where we were—then I grabbed the wrong leg and the step didn't work. Afterward, people came backstage and said they had known it was not a good pas de deux but hadn't realized it was so bad. I was really depressed. The audience didn't notice what went wrong because we handled it professionally, but what we did had nothing to do with the choreography.

"There was a funny incident when I danced with Margot [Fonteyn] in Puerto Rico. We were scheduled to dance at the university, but when we arrived they were on strike. There was no other occasion when Margot could have danced because she was too busy, so an emergency stage was erected in the convention center at the Holiday Inn. Unfortunately, the chandeliers came so low that once when I lifted Margot she got caught in one of them. I kept running, and then I realized she was not in my hand and I turned round to see her hanging from the chandelier. I went back and grabbed her, but I don't think I've ever laughed so hard as I did on that occasion.

"Another time we did *La Sylphide* together in Australia, with the Scottish Ballet. The set is very different to the one at [American] Ballet Theatre. Here, at the appropriate moment, I just open the window and the Sylphide steps onto the table, then the bench, and then steps down. On this occasion we had a set where the window was very high—it was more like a barn than a home—and the Sylphide has to step onto a mechanical lift which is then lowered. As she lands, I am then meant to try and touch her and she runs away. As she stepped through the window onto the lift, it just came down so drastically I thought she would break her neck, and the words she let out weren't quite those you would expect to hear from such an ethereal character. It is a standard joke with that ballet that James

Starr Danias and Rudolf Nureyev in the Joffrey Ballet's staging of Le Spectre de la Rose *for "Homage to Diaghilev."*

[the hero] is supposed to be stupid, because when the Sylphide arrives through the window his attitude is one of complete surprise. When she arrived so much earlier than expected I said with lightning speed, 'You-here-what-are-you-doing?' The atmosphere is meant to be very serious because the Sylphide is heartbroken, having discovered that James is going to marry his girlfriend, Effie. She is supposed to be crying, and we could not stop laughing. We tried so hard to control it and carry on, but sometimes when something sets you off you can get out of character. Also, laughing is counterproductive because it makes you so weak you can't lift."

After a performance of Petrouchka *with the Joffrey Ballet, Starr Danias and Rudolf Nureyev in his dressing room, together with Michael York.*

Anthony Dowell spoke of an appearance in Washington. "I was performing *Nutcracker* with Gelsey [Kirkland], who was unable to finish, so Rebecca Wright came on in the second act. She had done it before, but there had been a gap of about five months. Also, she had just had a week off, so she was a little unnerved by it all. There is one lovely part in the 'Waltz of the Flowers' where Clara and [the Prince] cross, go back again, cross once more, and then before exiting they cross for the last time. As we were doing this, I could see she was on a collision course. It was like the story of the two jet planes, that once you see the whites of the [other passengers'] eyes, you know you're going to collide. We were just drawn." At this point he let out a loud gasp, pounding one fist into the palm of his other hand to illustrate the force of impact. "The audience loved that one!"

Peter Martins talked of his experiences. "I've had some disasters. When I first came here I learned too many ballets in too short a time. Several ballets took one day and I performed them the same night. Only if I was lucky would I learn them one day and not have to perform them until the next. In the beginning, I never worked on anything on the stage, and that was tough. I learned very quickly—I can absorb a ballet in a couple of hours—but I don't have a high retention. Due to the way the New York City Ballet schedule is organized I would sometimes perform a ballet once, then have a two-week interval during which time I did not even rehearse it. Consequently, when I had to dance in any particular ballet for the second time it was like a new ballet. There was one unfortunate performance of *Brahms-Schoenberg Quartet*. I was dancing with Suzanne [Farrell] and I had five entrances and exits. Four of them went fine, then on the fifth occasion I forgot to enter. Suzanne was onstage and I was meant to come running out of the wings as she did piqué arabesque and took my hand. Well, my hand wasn't there! She fell, and I didn't even come and help her because I was out in the wings and didn't see what had happened. I wasn't even looking at the stage because I thought I had finished. Of course, from the audience's point of view it just looked like she had fallen. She was furious with me about that for a whole week."

Bart Cook recalled having taken a wrong exit at the New York State Theater during one performance. "There is a section in [*Tchaikovsky*] *Suite No. 3* where I back off the stage into the wings. Instead of looking at the line on the stage I was watching Sally [Sara Leland] and I backed off in the wrong place. I had to be upstage in sixteen counts. The problem was that I was stuck by the proscenium and the only way I could have got round it was by presenting myself in front of the audience in the same way I had come off. I saw a hole and there was a light coming down it, so I went through it. It was for wires and I'm sure it was only about one foot square. I literally crawled between the stage manager's legs and barely made it back to the stage. I was covered in dust and laughing very hard when I got there.

"On another occasion I had to do a part in *Dances at a Gathering* that usually I don't do. There is a point where one girl is dancing with three boys. The first one waltzes with her, the second throws her up, and the third catches her. The girl

New York City Ballet
principal Sean Lavery
performs with soloists Judith
Fugate and Robert Maiorano
in Jerome Robbins's Dances
at a Gathering.

was Sally and she was coming through the air doing a double tour, and I was too close so she passed me! I had to run and catch her, and barely made it—almost falling into the orchestra pit from the impact of her weight against me. That was frightening—I thought we were both going to hit the floor in a heap. It didn't show up too well in the review, either. One critic, I think it was Clive Barnes, said something to the effect that she and I had a joint Kamikaze pact. That really could have been a fiasco."

6

Company Life

A professional ballet company is comparable to a monastery, in terms of the dedication and single-mindedness it demands from its members. The unattainable perfection for which a dancer strives is his artistic high altar, and the stage his place of worship. His sackcloth is the daily physical grind, and he is chastised with a thousand disappointments, large and small, that are inherent in the life of any performer. Yet, if he is talented, the rewards of such dedication are improved performances, the praise of colleagues, audience appreciation, and, possibly, fame.

On entering a company, a dancer learns he must fend for himself. He is expected to produce good results in the same way as a corporate executive, and knows that if he does not prove beneficial to the company, he is equally dispensable. Dedicated performers are, of necessity, solitary people, and if they wish to attain any degree of success, their devotion to their art must come before all else. For those not involved, dancers often can be hard to understand, and anyone closely associated with dancers can find them very difficult to live with.

A ballet company is as political as any business or corporation. While the latter can survive only by making a profit, the former must produce consistently high standards before the public in order to convince both private and government sponsors that the company should be kept in existence. The budget required to maintain even a small dance company is exorbitant, and the majority of them live in permanent fear of inadequate funding. If there is a lack of money, a company cannot pay its dancers a reasonable salary and they may be able to maintain the company for relatively few performances a year, preceded by two or three weeks of rehearsal. This often means that a company has a high turnover of dancers, many of whom previously never have worked together during any given season. To reach high standards and then to maintain them requires constant hard work. Precision in a corps de ballet demands daily rehearsals, and a well-schooled ensemble is exciting to an audience, since its members are likely to be self-assured and capable of performing with a sense of urgency. If a group of dancers is to be able to attack each move with confidence, they must be certain of what they are doing.

Elena Tchernichova, a former member of the Kirov Ballet, is currently ballet mistress with American Ballet Theatre. Prior to the premiere of American Ballet Theatre's production of the full-length *La Bayadère* at the Metropolitan Opera House, she worked every day for a month with the twenty-four girls in the corps de ballet on the "Shades Scene" in the second act. The ballet was new to the West, but the "Shades Scene" is well known. The standard the corps reached was such that on opening night the audience was dazzled by their superior ability. There were nine consecutive performances of the ballet, during which time the high level of technique and artistry in that scene was maintained. The dancers then were obliged to perform other ballets in the repertoire and no time could be found for further rehearsals of the "Shades Scene." Consequently, when *La Bayadère* was performed later that New York season, the breathtaking accuracy was gone, the electricity in the air was missing, and the performances seemed to lack energy. No doubt the dancers, sensing that something had been lost, and understanding why, were not able to give their hearts and souls to the performance as they had been able to do given the confidence of regular rehearsals. Miss Tchernichova spoke afterward of the frustration that is caused by the need to maintain the high standards that are required for any particular ballet. If the company's repertoire were exclusively classical, the advantage would be that the dancers would be moving constantly in that style. However, some dancers are also involved in the works of Glen Tetley and other contemporary choreographers, and such ballets require a totally different technique. While it is difficult to give classical performances at night when rehearsing only contemporary works by day, it is also difficult for a performer to have the right feeling in his body for a contemporary piece if he has spent the whole day rehearsing classical ballet. Although it might be less interesting for the dancers, it would be ideal if a company could maintain those who danced exclusively classical and others who danced only contemporary works. Unfortunately, even for American Ballet Theatre, such luxuries are financially impossible.

Being a member of a ballet company requires leading a life-style molded to the profession. As dancers spend most of their waking hours working together, and possibly several months of the year traveling, relationships that develop can be very intense, and the closed environment can cause any degree of feeling to be unduly magnified. Owing to the fragile nature of a performer's emotions, love affairs formed within a company are sometimes short-lived, occasionally because of a third party, and the rejected person probably sees a former lover daily and perhaps is obliged also to continue with a performing partnership. Such experiences can be insufferably painful.

If a dancer has spent all his professional life as a member of one company and then moves to another, grafting himself onto the new company requires some readjustment. Anthony Dowell discovered this when, having already acquired an international reputation with his home company, the Royal Ballet, he took a leave of absence to join American Ballet Theatre for one year, to broaden his experience. "I had to adjust to feeling like a new boy at school, and it took a while before I started to feel a part of them. I hadn't bargained for feeling so much like an outsider, while so desperately wanting to belong. Also, during the ten weeks of rehearsal between September and December, there was no end product, and without performing it made it very hard because I had nothing to hang on to. I even lacked so many of the normal outlets. If I wanted to lose myself, there was no point in buying a picture or a mirror, because I didn't even have my own apartment." However, being able to exist on his own, he feels, is a very important quality, if not a good one. "It is lonely," mused Mr. Dowell. "That is a grand statement to make, but the moment comes, after you've had your teachers and friends bolstering you, when suddenly you are in your costume and standing in the wings. That's it. Everything is up to you." If a dancer makes a conscious decision to be alone after a performance it can often be misread and cause offense, and is also contrary to the image most people have of a famous dancer's life. "I do feel sometimes they think that life is one long continuous party, which simply isn't the case."

People have always needed idols who were far removed from them. Until comparatively recently, dancers were rarely seen before the public except onstage and very little was widely known about their lives. Many who pursue famous artists do so on a superficial level, knowing of an idol only what is seen in performance, and remaining completely unaware of the personality involved. "Even though I'm in the business," said Anthony Dowell, "I'm fascinated by other people in the profession. It does have a certain glamour about it. Where outsiders are concerned, in the early stages of meeting someone you just have to be cautious, and I am wary until I find out what it is that attracts them."

Dennis Nahat spoke of three stars whom he found intriguing to work with.

"Baryshnikov to me is the epitome of what any dancer should be because he can do any style much more naturally than any other dancer—even Nureyev. He doesn't have the aura that Rudi has, simply because of his physical appearance. To start with, he's a smaller man. Nureyev has that aura of mysticism about him and that aristocratic-looking face. You don't touch Nureyev when you pass him by, but Mischa you can touch because he has a different personality. He's more vulnerable. Nureyev will throw his snoot up in the air and walk away from you. If Mischa does that you laugh at him because he doesn't emanate aristocraticism. Erik Bruhn is the same as Nureyev. They are the princes. You don't touch a prince—you stand back and admire."

Rudolf Nureyev has been much cited by the press for his emotional outbursts, and Leslie Caron, who worked with him in the film *Valentino* (about the life of Rudolph Valentino), talked of that experience. "He is unique, amazingly courageous, and very generous. Also he is a true genius and extremely sensitive, and I don't think the press do him justice. He's not temperamental, just honest! If somebody maligns him, adversely affects a performance, or is jealous—which often happens to him—he fights like a demon, and is as direct as a tank. Once at a party after a performance, I saw a woman tell him she didn't think the program had been done in the right order. He lashed out at her without mincing his words. It was wonderful."

Peter Martins talked on the subject of fans. "When you leave the theatre at night you are slightly hassled. I understand, though. If fifteen people want autographs, I stop and sign my name for them all, because I think back to the times I wanted autographs. I don't like to be pursued into a restaurant, because I consider that my privacy, although even then I don't have the heart to tell them to leave me alone and I give them my autograph. I remember one woman who consistently wrote me marriage proposals. She would include her picture and did not leave me alone for about two years, although I never encouraged her. I never even answered any of her letters. She pursued me everywhere. Finally, one day a letter came to the theatre together with a photograph of myself torn up. That was the end!"

American Ballet Theatre attracts audiences on the basis of who is dancing rather than what is being danced. At the New York City Ballet, there is a "no-star" system and audiences go to see particular ballets. A week's casting is made public only at the beginning of that week. Peter Martins responded to being asked what he thinks are the advantages of the "no-star" system.

"I don't believe there are no stars, and I don't mean that in the sense that it sounds! I agree totally with Balanchine on his theory, because you have only to look at companies to see why he thinks that way. American Ballet Theatre depends on a few individual dancers who happen to be the public's favorites. That's frightening. You can't run an artistic institution on that level. As we all know, Balanchine makes the point that he wants the ballets to sell. There is so much talent [at the New York City Ballet] and dancing is comparable to acting. A good actor needs demanding roles. So it is with dancers, and Balanchine has the right combination in this company. He has all the good ballets which attract talented people. Now look at Ballet Theatre. Obviously the classics are great ballets, but the twentieth-century repertoire is not so impressive. Practically every talented dancer wants to try this company [New York City Ballet]. They don't all want to stay, because it's not right for everybody. Peter Schaufuss didn't like it. He left for the National Ballet of Canada, because he found he functioned better with them."

The well-known principal ballet dancers, and also some soloists, do guest performances with other companies, internationally and around the country. Sometimes they go as individuals and on other occasions with a chosen partner. Within reason, fees are based on what sponsors are able to afford, and dancers will accept bookings as much as one or two years in advance. This can have its disadvantages. A dancer often will look in his diary, find he has three to five days during a season in which he is not scheduled to perform with his home company, and accept an engagement, be it in Baltimore or Chicago. He will possibly leave his home company the morning after a performance and return only the day before another. On paper this looks easy, and only when the situation arises does the dancer stop to think that maybe he has overloaded his schedule. Sometimes extra performances will be in the summer, when dancers have had very little free time since the previous fall. Toward the end of a summer season they tend to be overtired, and to have to fit in extra performances and spend hours sitting on an airplane can really be most unwelcome when the time comes.

Occasionally, misadventure causes schedules to conflict at the last minute, and a dancer may have to request permission to miss a performance with his own company so as to be able to save a smaller company from a crisis. On a Friday night at the end of one summer season with the New York City Ballet, Peter Martins was to perform in *Chaconne* with his home company. That weekend, he was also to dance with the Stars of the Royal Danish Ballet, then appearing at City Center in New York. Meanwhile, Robert Weiss had choreographed a ballet entitled *The Birds,* and had set the pas de deux on Peter Martins and Kay Mazzo. The ballet was being performed over two weekends at the annual festival in Caramoor, about an hour's drive from New York City. Mr. Martins was to appear in the first weekend's performances only, and Mr. Weiss was due to dance the second weekend. Unfortunately, Mr. Weiss suffered an injury that prevented him from performing, and the only other dancer who knew the role was Mr. Martins. On the Friday evening, Adam Lüders replaced Mr. Martins in *Chaconne* at the New York City Ballet, and on Friday and Saturday evenings Mr. Martins was driven up to Caramoor after a full day's rehearsal so that he could perform each night. Not only did Mr. Martins have to rehearse ballets in which he was dancing, but he was also in the process of choreographing on Bart Cook and Heather Watts the pas de deux from *Sonate di Scarlatti*, his ballet due to be premiered during the New York City Ballet's summer season at Saratoga Springs, New York, about two weeks later. He was scheduled to appear with the Danes on the Sunday evening, and then because of an injury to one of them on the Saturday evening he was asked to make an extra appearance at City Center. The ballet in which he danced was changed from last to first on the evening's program. After performing it Mr. Martins was driven posthaste to Caramoor, where he appeared in *The Birds*, which had been scheduled last that night. During the day on Saturday he had to rehearse also with Natalia Makarova at American Ballet Theatre for a future guest performance with another company.

(Although it is necessary to have talent and good training to be accepted into a leading dance company, it is equally important to be liked by ballet masters, choreographers, and, especially, the company director.) If one is a member of a company whose director has a penchant for tall blonds, being a short brunette might be detrimental to promotion, unless the dancer is in some way unique. Sometimes a corps de ballet member watches the scheduling week after week, hoping for roles for which he feels suited, and maybe for which he has even asked. When he is continually not cast he remains in the corps, often working hard, yet being given little to do. In such circumstances, it is very difficult for a dancer to keep up his spirits. Possibly, once a year he is given a solo role and is expected to give an outstanding performance, despite being under such pressure. The dancer considers himself to be under scrutiny, and since it usually takes several performances of a role for any dancer to feel comfortable in it, he is unlikely to perform up to his full potential on the first occasion. Naturally, those who have resisted casting the dancer then are dissatisfied.

It can be equally demoralizing for a dancer to have to rehearse a role and then never be cast in it. Sometimes a young company member is used as a substitute for a principal or star in rehearsals, or even certain performances. If he allows himself to be sufficiently exploited, he may eventually be so overworked that he then suffers from chronic injuries to the point where he can no longer perform.

There is a very fine line between opportunity and exploitation, and it is not always possible for a dancer to tell which situation he is in.

Some dancers, disillusioned with the politics involved in company life, fall into a rut. There is a reasonable turnover in most companies—some dancers make the mistake of leaving prematurely, while others hang on too long in the hopes that their situation will improve.

It is unfortunate when a dancer cannot recognize that he will never be promoted. If he is no longer needed, frequently his roles will be taken away, and then he will leave. Occasionally the women marry doctors because, due to their life-style, those are among the few men they meet. Some dancers teach. Elise Flagg was a New York City Ballet corps member for ten years before she left to join the Zurich Ballet. The company is directed by sisters Pat and Colleen Neary, both former members of the New York City Ballet. Miss Flagg joined the Zurich Ballet as soloist, and eighteen months later appeared with the company in London, partnered by Rudolf Nureyev in Balanchine's *Rubies*. She was promoted to principal after the London tour.

Conversely, certain young dancers lose patience and in a moment of anger feel like resigning. Peter Martins almost left the New York City Ballet on two occasions. "Both times I called up SAS and made reservations home to Denmark. The first time, I think, was after one year of being here. There was one week left of the season and I booked a one-way ticket. After sleeping on it for a couple of nights, I realized that was being self-indulgent, and decided to stick with it. The other time, I decided to leave after a fight with Balanchine. It appeared he did not want me to be what I am, because he really attacked me. He said I had come here thinking I owned the world and that because I had the fifth position and could do nice pirouettes to the right and left, I thought that everything should stop for me. He told me it wasn't the way he worked and that if I wanted to leave, nobody was going to stop me. Then he informed me that he had other dancers who could take my place without any problem. By that time I had been with the company for about three or four years. I already had a large repertoire and had asked for a part that he would not give me. I asked him why, and he told me I was not good enough! Then I challenged him and asked if he thought the person he was casting was better than me. I was brusquely told it didn't matter how good the other man was, I was not good enough. He then went on to explain that the other dancer and I were not of the same standard, and obviously he expected more of me. I had made the great mistake of cornering him, which is fatal. I learned my lesson. I realized that if I didn't do things his way, I might as well leave the company, because he would make it impossible for me to stay. I pass that advice on to all the young dancers, too. I swallowed my pride, but realized very fast what he was doing. I'm very perceptive and sensed that whenever he put me down there had to be a good reason for it. After all, who was I to think I was such a good dancer! I realized I needed to learn many things. Finally, he told me that if I wanted to stay with the company he would teach me and work with me whenever I wanted him to but that I should not try to give the impression that I already know so much. He was very honest with me!"

As there are so many talented dancers available, a director can afford to be selective, and promotion tends to be less rapid now than in days gone by. Robert Weiss agrees with this. "I think it is healthy for a dancer to be promoted slowly. He should be able to cope with the company politics and other day-to-day problems. You have to be aware of who you are." Merrill Ashley mentioned the disadvantages of premature promotion. "Mr. Balanchine has been burned several times, feeling that he's promoted some people too early. If this happens, they either don't develop the way he expected, or they regress, and he is left with a dancer he doesn't know how to use. He's very loyal; he would never fire anybody, but they are earning a good salary that could be given to somebody else. So in recent years I think he has been waiting until dancers are overly ready for promotion."

When a dancer is called to perform in an emergency, if he is caught at a bad moment it can be alarming, and Steven Caras has suffered such an experience. "One free evening I was at home with friends and we were relaxing and enjoying ourselves. At about nine o'clock, when dance was very far from my mind, the phone rang. The ballet mistress was on the line to say that a boy who had replaced me in *Symphony in Three Movements* was suffering from muscle spasms in his back and that I was needed to do the ballet. I asked her if she could prepare my things and she said that she would. Hastily, I came back with the fact that I was nervous, to be informed that they would do everything they could to help me. Then I told her I would shave quickly and be on my way—which I was before I knew it. It was raining very heavily, so I had to trudge my way through puddles." (Suddenly one pictures Gene Kelly's delightful scene, "dancing and singing in the rain.")

"*Symphony in Three Movements* is a very hard ballet, and fortunately when I arrived in the boys' dressing room, my makeup was set up for me. The ballet mistress went into my theatre case and found shoes for me, and poor Jay Jolley was lying on his back on the floor with the company doctor tending to him. As I started to make up I had a timid smile on my face. Then I got dressed fast, though somewhat hampered by my nervousness, and my colleagues asked me why I did not go down to the stage to warm up. The ballet prior to *Symphony in Three Movements* had almost finished and there was only a few minutes' pause before I had to go on. My answer to them was simply that I was warm purely from anticipation of what lay ahead, which shows I didn't even know what I was saying. I finally had no time to warm up, but I think my body was still warm from rushing to the theatre. I had a great time. Everything went off all right except for one moment where five couples are involved in a lift and my partner and I didn't connect on time. I gestured with my hands as if lifting her into the air, which must have looked very strange, but I was very careful to make sure I was lined up with the boy in front of me, so I'm not sure quite what went wrong. I was glad it was possible for me to go on in an emergency. The company was very appreciative and I was pleased to be able to do it for them. That is the one time I have been caught that way, because luckily I've always had reasonable notice when substituting for another dancer."

Although numbers tend to vary slightly from season to season, American Ballet Theatre and New York City Ballet both have approximately a hundred dancers. Without efficient organization and strict discipline, such companies would be unable to function. The Joffrey Ballet currently has thirty-five dancers, but Mr. Joffrey always has ruled with a firm hand, a principle on which Scott Barnard supports him. "There seems to be some resistance to discipline at the moment, but it will swing back again, because otherwise companies fall apart. It's been very frustrating for me over the past few years because dancers have become increasingly independent. If they offer resistance, I think they have to be let go. You can perhaps allow a company of eight people to 'do their thing,' but in a company any larger than that there will be problems. Mr. Joffrey likes everyone to be on the same plane when we are traveling, and I agree with him. You cannot have situations where a dancer gets mad and flies out or refuses to perform. When dancers are disciplined and have people to look after them it gives them confidence. If you want a slick-looking company the dancers must be together on everything and they must be advised. It is particularly selfish for dancers to stubbornly refuse to do what they are asked in a role, because if a ballet does not look good overall, their behavior is self-defeating. If they persist and the ballet is subsequently pulled out of the repertoire, they are left without a role."

Even in the large companies, dancers are frequently cast in several successive performances. It is not unusual for them to be in seven or eight performances a week, for which they must learn to pace themselves, in order to build the necessary stamina. If they do three ballets a performance, eventually they become accustomed to it. As Mr. Barnard stated, "Usually dancers are at their best when they can do the hard roles and appear relaxed. When they have the stamina, it becomes almost easy to them."

While performing and/or rehearsing, dancers need as much sleep and rest as they can fit into their schedules. On a day off, they sometimes sleep for the entire time, or at least stay off their feet, reading or watching television. At the end of one New York City Ballet season at Kennedy Center in Washington, D.C., Bart Cook slept for a day and a half upon returning to New York City. The stage at Kennedy Center is notoriously hard, and on the final Saturday and Sunday Mr. Cook had danced in all four performances. A week later he felt his body was still in shock from dancing on the hard stage.

Maria Calegari is now a soloist with the New York City Ballet, but she talked of her daily routine while still a corps member. "I wake up at about eight-thirty, eat breakfast, which is usually a hard-boiled egg and lots of coffee, and read the paper. You have to go to the theatre looking presentable for class, especially when Mr. B. teaches, so that means doing your hair neatly. I also put makeup on. You have to decide what to wear depending on your mood, and then class is usually at eleven for an hour. Mr. Balanchine's classes are extremely difficult, and even if he isn't teaching it's still hard because you are dealing with yourself. Sometimes it's easier with him, if only because he is so inspiring he takes your mind off yourself. After class you sometimes rehearse from noon to six, although union regulations stipulate that we are not allowed to rehearse for more than three hours together. Usually that evening's ballets are rehearsed onstage and the others in the studios. It depends on the time of the season as to how long you have off in the afternoons, but it's usually between one and two hours. If you have two or occasionally three hours off, you can either go home or shop, or just collapse and read. I personally find I can't separate myself from the theatre and if I go home before a performance I can't get back into the swing very easily. I go out and get something to eat and bring it back. Maybe as I get older I will change, and it will probably be a good idea if I do, if only for health reasons, but at the moment I find it too difficult. During the periods we are laid off, I find life very hard because I don't have many outside contacts and don't really know how to deal effectively with free time. I also get totally disenchanted with the outside world. I have to relearn many things. Even going shopping gets to me!"

Such an attitude is not unusual for young dancers who have been with a company for one or two years, since achieving the high standards needed to remain in a company leaves little time to do anything but dance. However, once they become veterans, dancers normally change their outlook. Greg Huffman feels acutely that to allow dance to become an obsession is self-defeating. "I see many dancers taking themselves so seriously and coming offstage upset thinking they did a terrible performance. (Frequently I have seen that performance and thought it went very well!) When you become obsessed with dance you lose your sense of perspective about it. It is essential to get away from it sometimes, whether to look at mountains in Switzerland or just to read or visit a park. If you don't experience other things it really affects your performances. To project something honestly—to feel like you're in a wonderful glade—you have to have had that experience. There are people who go to the theatre every day, even if they don't have rehearsals. They go home at night to rinse out their tights, then return the next morning to start all over again. Dance is a way of life, but I don't feel you can cut yourself off from the rest of the world as if it did not exist."

In the United States, companies that categorize their dancers divide them into three levels—Corps de Ballet, Soloists, and Principals. Some of the smaller companies are not ranked, but are listed alphabetically as, due to lack of numbers, dancers must do both solo and ensemble work. American Ballet Theatre and New York City Ballet dancers are ranked. Of the smaller companies, so, for example, is the Houston Ballet, whereas the Joffrey Ballet, Cleveland Ballet, and Pennsylvania Ballet are not. These four companies currently have fewer than forty dancers. The Joffrey Ballet has sixteen women and nineteen men, and the other three companies each have four more women than men. Companies outside the United States usually are divided into more than three categories. The Royal Ballet is divided into Artists, Coryphées, Solo Artists, and Principals. The Ballet Nacional de Cuba consists of Corps de Ballet, Coryphées, Soloists, Principals, and Premier Dancers.

The title "ballerina" refers to a female dancer of the highest distinction, but nowadays frequently is used incorrectly to describe any female dancer. A girl of lesser rank is a "ballet dancer," a title that in itself carries great merit. Although a first-ranking male dancer is referred to as a "premier danseur," there is another title, "danseur noble," which applies to a man with many years of dancing experience who has both excellent classical ballet technique and artistry and aristocratic bearing. Contemporary danseurs nobles are Rudolf Nureyev, Vladimir Vassiliev (of the Bolshoi Ballet), Anthony Dowell, and Fernando Bujones. While still dancing, Erik Bruhn and Ivan Nagy were two more examples.

In the West, it was not until about the latter half of the 1960s that men started to play a prominent role in ballet. Prior to that, audiences went to a performance to see the scheduled ballerina, and normally were concerned only minimally with whoever partnered her. Society found it difficult to accept men dressed in tights who performed the refined movements inherent in ballet, and many potential audience members stayed away. When Rudolf Nureyev left the Soviet Union to dance in the West, attitudes changed. Audiences at last saw how much excitement a male dancer could generate. The popularity of men in ballet has now grown to such an extent that the late 1970s and early 1980s have become the era of the male dancer.

American Ballet Theatre and the New York City Ballet are probably the only two ballet companies in the United States whose dancers can consider themselves fully employed. Although bookings obviously vary from year to year, neither company usually has more than six to eight weeks annually when not performing or at least rehearsing. There is no pay during a nonworking week. Salaries for the majority of other dancers range from inadequate to almost token payments, and most would not be able to dance without other means of support. Even corps members in the country's two principal companies are adequately paid, but due to the star system at American Ballet Theatre and the no-star system at the New York City Ballet, there is a vast difference between the two companies in the amount earned by a principal dancer. A long-standing principal or star in the former company is purported to earn $8,000 a week, whereas even the top dancers at the New York City Ballet earn only $1,500 a week when performing and half of that during rehearsal weeks with their home company. Very few dancers become wealthy from dance, or even earn the equivalent of their corporate counterparts.

Superstition is as much a part of ballet folklore as other aspects of life. To wish a performer good luck before going onstage is considered bad luck, although nowadays the term is becoming more acceptable. It has been suggested that offering good luck implies that an individual is likely to need it, and so other expressions have evolved. "Break a leg," an actor would say to a colleague, although this way of expressing one's good wishes to a dancer seems somewhat inappropriate, and one of the most commonly used salutations is "merde." As it is the French word for "shit," it is difficult to conclude how it came to be used to express good luck, but it is commonly heard around dressing rooms before a performance. Nowadays dancers are less prone to cling to the traditional superstitions, but some, such as whistling backstage, still cause a certain amount of discomfort.

Ballet is now seen on film with increasing frequency. Sometimes a live performance is broadcast on television, in which case it is captured forever and dancers have no opportunity to correct mistakes. On occasion ballets are either adapted for television, originally choreographed for the medium, or used in feature films. Although usually an interesting experience for dancers, a film sometime takes them away from dance for months, and the time that is being missed can cause frustration. A section of a scene may take a full day to shoot, and a dancer can be required to do a three-minute piece many times before the director considers he has a good take. For this, the dancer must keep warm as long as he is filming, so that as soon as he has finished one take he goes off camera and exercises at the barre until he is needed for the next take. There is little time for sitting down.

New York City Ballet is frequently filmed by the Public Broadcasting Service, and Kay Mazzo found difficulty in working within the reduced area necessary to enable the cameras to give the best coverage. "When you're used to being on an enormous stage and suddenly have only six feet to work in, you feel as if you're not even dancing. As a dancer I feel that the cameraman cannot have the correct perspective, although I think they are improving. Usually Mr. Balanchine is there editing and offering guidance, and he has a good eye, but there are still unavoidable limitations. Constant repetition can be very frustrating. I think dancers are like sprinters. You go out and do a variation and it's over, but for film you do it a little at a time, which is even tougher. Many years ago we filmed *Serenade* in Berlin in several sections. When I saw it afterward, it seemed to me that the ballet had no flow at all. Sometimes you can go straight through a ballet, which is much better, because then at least it feels like a performance."

In 1933, Alicia Markova was one of the first ballerinas to dance for television. Performances lasted about ten minutes, were open to the public, and were given in major department stores in London over closed-circuit television, as it was still not broadcast. Dame Alicia talked of the experience. "There was almost no space," she said, indicating an area of her London sitting room about ten by fourteen feet. "Yet one had to try and give the impression that one was moving. A strong light flashed from the camera, which was only a few feet away, so to keep one's balance was very difficult. The floor was marked in black-and-white squares and all of one's theatre costume was outlined in black. The original television makeup was a very white face with a black mouth and purple eyes. There was a piano accompaniment, and I remember on one occasion, when I had finished the variation, to come out of view I had to duck down on the floor and crawl out under the piano."

The filming of dance has its controversial aspects; when the two art forms, dance and film, are brought together, both have to be somewhat compromised. Usually the camera is either too close or too far back. Ballet is a very refined art, and the acting and mime are very subtle, so if the camera is too far away, that is missed. Alternatively, if it is shot from up close, it becomes too intimate, and the overall illusion is lost.

Ballets are often adapted to some extent for the camera, which in turn is compromised because it is used as an instrument to deliver dance in the best possible fashion to the audience, rather than having the free range that its own enormous capacity affords.

Scott Barnard's belief is that "dance is magic, which cannot be put in a two-dimensional form and improved upon. The electricity that goes through the air when the conductor starts the overture is not there. An artificial rose is still artificial, even if it is silk. It is beautiful and from a distance it's convincing, but it is not the same as the real thing."

The feature film *The Turning Point* starred Mikhail Baryshnikov as Yuri and Leslie Browne as Amelia, his ballet partner and girlfriend. Starr Danias played the role of Carolyn, who lures Yuri into a brief romantic diversion, and Miss Danias recalls the scene in which Amelia is learning the role of Juliet. Yuri, who will dance Romeo, looks over at Amelia and the two make eye contact, marking the moment at which their romance begins. Carolyn is working at the barre in the background during filming, and Miss Danias was obliged to maintain the feat for an entire day. It did much to perfect her technique, she said, and by evening she managed to hold her balance for ten minutes.

In August 1980, Thames Television (which broadcasts from London during weekdays) aired the Royal Ballet's production of *Swan Lake*. John Michael Phillips directed, and later he spoke of some of the problems involved in presenting the ballet for television. The performance was shot on videotape using eight cameras, which, as it was done at the Royal Opera House, had to be placed in the specific areas wired for the purpose. The audience's sight lines had to be kept clear, and cameras could not be placed onstage or other cameras would have picked them up. A dancer's line is presented to the front of a house and the line is lost if shot with a camera set at the wrong angle. The camera is further limited since, for example, it cannot peer into the wings. If it did, while covering the performance, it might pick up stagehands in the background. Stage lighting presents a problem, as it is not bright enough for color, and when the cameramen were obliged to use the bottom end of the cameras' range, to keep the picture from becoming muddy, certain scenes had to be differently lit. For example, lighting that gives a dappled effect onstage is ideal in a theatre but does not work on camera. Consequently, Thames's lighting technician and the lighting designer for *Swan Lake* worked together to produce the levels of illumination necessary, without altering the intent of the lighting. When directing, Mr. Phillips worked from a camera script marked down to the nearest note, which was written from a black-and-white videotape the Royal Ballet lent Thames Television.

Audiences are educated by television to expect different angles and other variations in shots that in some way enhance the drama, comedy, or other form of entertainment they are watching. They are not used to seeing dull shots. Television viewers are not necessarily balletgoers, and therefore are less concerned with the precision in the steps than with action, interesting pictures, and the story. In a theatre, the human eye's peripheral vision picks up the visual aspect of the total illusion. When looking at television, although the eye picks up the televised subject matter, peripherally it also takes in whatever is in its range, which detracts from the specific atmosphere required by *Swan Lake*. However, treated in the right way, Mr. Phillips believes, television should be able to add to ballet's aura, rather than detract from it. The debate as to the effectiveness of dance on film and television continues.

The union that represents dancers in the United States is the American Guild of Musical Artists (AGMA). Not all dance companies are members, but as they reach a certain status they are encouraged to join. AGMA stipulates minimum salaries and sets working conditions. For example, stages must comply with certain standards, and performing out-of-doors is not officially permitted in temperatures below fifty-five degrees. This sometimes occurs, unless the dancers involved make a stand, and there are occasions when they perform at outdoor theatres in cool temperatures and steam can be seen rising from their bodies, while the audience sits wrapped in blankets.

Member companies of AGMA have representatives within them, and the number varies according to the size of the company. In all areas of society, unions and management have their own interests at heart, and strikes resulting from lack of compromise on either side are commonplace. This is true also of the powerful ballet companies, though smaller ones are not prepared to risk their future. The demands that American Ballet Theatre members made against management in 1979 almost caused the company to close down. Although the concessions asked for did not concern the stars, several supported the demands, either verbally or by their presence at demonstrations. On one occasion, Gelsey Kirkland appeared displaying a placard that read THESE FEET WEREN'T MADE FOR WALKING. Ultimately, the dancers were granted most of the concessions for which they asked, although negotiations became particularly unpleasant because the dancers were forbidden to work until a settlement was reached. The fall rehearsal period (normally about ten weeks long) was lost, and the company's appearance in Washington, D.C., which normally takes place in December, had to be cancelled. After a month of rehearsals, the company was onstage again in January 1980.

Greg Huffman mentioned some of the difficulties with which dancers can be faced. "The companies would not want to admit it, but they can make your life very difficult. If dancers insist on the five-minute break or raise another particular point that is our right, they are looked down upon by the ballet masters, management, and the board of directors. They may not say anything, but maybe they'll show you how they feel by not giving you a part you want. This makes the dancers feel insecure. They can't be fired, but they can be held back. I do not have the time to be a union representative and I don't want the responsibility, but there are things that are wrong. We complain amongst ourselves, without making our feelings known to management. They work us to death. We do get paid for it, but most of those hours are unnecessary. They may do a run-through of a very hard ballet at six or seven in the evening, after five or six hours of rehearsal, and then expect to see us do it again in performance at eight. It's absurd and really insensitive. Many times you feel that you are just a machine—a body out there. Instead of refusing to do it, we keep going and then break down in tears, and they cannot understand what's wrong."

Unfortunately, because of limited funds, companies are constantly trying to obtain the most from the dancers they have, and this occasionally affects the level of artistry. Also, certain ballets that draw the public are presented principally because they are commercial. However, as such ballets attract large audiences, companies are more easily able to justify presenting ballets of high quality that appeal, sometimes, to only comparatively few balletgoers.

7

Home Life

The total dedication that is required of ballet dancers can be perceived, sometimes, as pure selfishness rather than single-mindedness by those living close to them.

When onstage, performers are not only aiming for expertise, they are also satisfying a deeply rooted emotional need. While being able to lose themselves in the actions and emotions of the moment, they also need to be admired. An audience is "safe." Its members admire from afar, and any individual performer cultivates his own followers. For the young corps de ballet member, his audience will initially be confined to family and friends, whereas well-known dancers fill theatres with members of the general public, and also attract equally famous people of diverse talents. That is theatrical life.

At home, a performer can frequently be introverted and regard hours offstage as interludes between performances. Fans who try to come too close to an idol are often disillusioned. Although usually treated courteously by a performer, some fans consider themselves friends of artists, and when an object of their admiration blows cold, his attitude is interpreted as rudeness.

Like many dancers, Peter Martins values his privacy highly. "Sometimes in my apartment, I open the shades to the sun and the neighbors look in. That makes me feel uncomfortable, so I put the shades down again. I like my privacy, and the only way I can get it sometimes is by being rude, which is very hard for me to do—not that I'm such a nice guy, it's just that I've been brought up differently. I give a little hint and hope they get it, but they don't. Then I start lying and they catch up with me. Finally, I get angry. It really is necessary to behave that way sometimes, but then you acquire a reputation for being arrogant."

Any individual who places great emphasis on his career can be difficult to live with, but in the artist the problems are often accentuated by emotional fragility. Ballet dancers are human beings of a very special nature, not only athletically refined but with a high degree of sensitivity. They are the human equivalent of foals born to Arab stallions and English mares, and Mr. Balanchine equates the dancers at the New York City Ballet with racehorses.

During performance periods, especially, many dancers will become totally absorbed in themselves, which from a lover's point of view can imply that a partner is withdrawing from a relationship. Most frequently, it represents a desire to be left alone, as possibly even the concentration necessary to carry on an interesting conversation would draw too much energy away from that which is of prime importance—the dance. The performer requires special understanding, but for those unfamiliar with the temperament, it can become unbearable. The need to be idolized onstage can be carried home, and the tolerance expected of a partner can put excessive strain on a relationship. Behavior is sometimes childish, but this stems mainly from the deeply rooted emotional insecurity inherent in all artists. While love remains blind, frequently the partner sees only a glamorous figure, and not until the aura disappears do the problems start.

Anthony Dowell elaborated. "I think it is hard getting emotionally involved with someone outside the business. Often they cannot understand what it entails, especially at my stage of the game, and when they first meet you, you are perceived as a glamorous figure. They see you in the papers and on television being interviewed, which all bolsters the aura. Then you start to lay yourself open, [exposing] your insecurities and worries, and they have a hard time trying to understand you. I think one is suddenly seen as a neurotic mess by them and they are not able to cope. That's the trouble with first impressions onstage. You are [seen as] successful, together, glamorous. I agree there is that element [that emanates from] any celebrity—a magic and electricity that does affect people. You just have to be cautious about emotional involvements, because people seem to feel 'How dare you be down when you're Anthony Dowell, a star!' "

Regarding personal involvements, Gary Chryst commented, "I find it totally impossible to maintain close relationships! It would require a very understanding mate in your field. Relationships can work, but only as long as you're not too demanding of each other."

The majority of people involved with performers usually are required to do most of the giving. A businessman married to a dancer who comes home at 11:00 P.M. and needs to relax and find dinner waiting, or be taken to a restaurant, needs to be of an unusual nature. If he can accept his wife's love of dance, and be happy that she is contented, a marriage can last, but the time may come when he would like to be able to eat at a reasonable hour and spend the evening with his wife. While living through a season's pressures, dancers often are unable to conceive of the troubles of others, and if a partner mentions a problem, his words may fall on deaf ears. When he finishes speaking, the answer he receives could be a reference to that day's problems at the theatre. Maybe on a performance day a dancer will receive a telephone call from a friend wishing to discuss a problem. Many cannot allow their minds to be distracted in this way, because it creates negative energy. It is physically and emotionally draining for a dancer to have to divert his energy away from an upcoming performance, to apply the concentration required for giving constructive advice at three o'clock if he must be onstage at eight.

Male dancers almost invariably marry or live with another dancer, because, despite the problems, ultimately there is a greater likelihood of mutual understanding than with a nondancer.

Shortly before the release of the film *Nijinsky* in the spring of 1980, Rebecca Wright spoke of her three-year relationship with George de la Peña, who played the title role. At the time, both of them were soloists with American Ballet Theatre. "It is difficult, because George is a beautiful-looking man, and very talented. On the other hand, I have had much more experience than he has, and am better known as a dancer. Despite that, George gets more recognition than I do in Ballet Theatre, and more opportunities. Essentially, that is because there are three girls to every man. Even though I can accept that intellectually, when things move quickly for him and slowly for me I get envious and feel frustrated. Bad things come out and he bears the brunt of that, which is very difficult in the relationship. Also, he is in a strong position in the dance world because the women are attracted to him and I have to fight hard not to be possessive and it's a fearful position to be in. I have to really work at believing in myself and trust in my own inner beauty and strength, which is extremely difficult to do. I am now able to be much more objective than before, but with George's pending success as a movie star there will be other problems, because people tend to dote on him as a celluloid figure to the extent of excluding me."

As there is a predominance of homosexuality or bisexuality among male dancers, and women outnumber men, most women must look outside the companies for their romantic attachments.

Due to their isolated lives, women sometimes have difficulty meeting men who are not connected with ballet, and those who remain in the companies for many years occasionally remain single. Those who meet marriageable men outside the companies frequently give up the dance to become housewives, either because the life-style and the travel involved can become a threat to a marriage, or because they no longer wish to perform. Many women who marry and remain within the companies either choose not to have children or have them only after they are thirty or even at forty, to enable them to devote their dancing years to their art form.

In the socialist countries, the situation is different. Homosexuals are not accepted into dance companies, and many dancers marry within their companies while still young. The women take the time required to have babies and then return to the dance.

Despite the unique understanding the temperament of the performer requires, there are many advantages to being closely associated with him. There are a number of ballet dancers who are happily married, or living with partners who follow their careers very closely. In many cases a partner attends a mate's performances regularly and will be both the most constructive critic and devoted fan. The thrill of a performance for an audience member who has a special bond with a dancer can be one of life's most exhilarating experiences. Knowing the moments the dancer finds particularly difficult can have the observer sitting on the edge of a seat; remembering certain anecdotes or jokes can cause a smile; and the knowledge of what the dancer has gone through to achieve the special tiny moments of satisfaction when he or she performs something with the perfect combination of technique and artistry can touch the dancer's most intimate ally more deeply than even the closest friend.

Both Ivan Nagy's first wife, in Hungary, and his present wife, Marilyn Burr, were dancers. "I'm not sure if I were married to someone outside ballet that she would be able to understand [certain aspects of what the life entails]," Mr. Nagy said, shortly before retiring. "We are in the touching business, and I go on tour for guest engagements with a partner. Although the relationship isn't physical, we do have a rapport, and I'd say I'm in love with Margot [Fonteyn], Natasha [Natalia Makarova], Cynthia [Gregory], and Gelsey [Kirkland]. That feeling has to exist, otherwise you can't project anything temporal. If I am to create something, I have to love the person I'm dancing with."

As Jean-Pierre Bonnefous was in the transitional period of building up his career as a choreographer, before retiring from the New York City Ballet, he discussed his marriage to Patricia McBride. "If each of you respects when the other is tired and needs to rest rather than go out and socialize, it's fine; otherwise it can become very difficult. Also, if competition exists between you it can be a problem. You have to balance the power you want to have at home and the power you need as a dancer. If something goes wrong at the personal or professional end it is very hard trying to keep the two separated. If a rehearsal doesn't go smoothly, we really have to be careful; otherwise we spend the whole evening in the same mood and it can be pretty heavy. It took us a few years to establish a balance." Miss McBride agreed: "In the early days of knowing each other we were only romantically involved, and it was not until later that we danced together. Then there was tension, which created a lot of drama, and we realized if we wanted a relationship, we would have to work hard at it. At first, we would take things so personally. If one criticized the other professionally, we didn't take it as we would from another partner. Now we look forward to working with each other, though, and things work really well."

Although Cynthia Gregory's husband is not a dancer, he is an artist. "He is a singer and songwriter. He manages me, and I'm very lucky because he understands artists very well. I have a tendency to be lazy and to think only about what I'm doing in ballet—to really get into my roles—and he'll pull me out of it. He helps me bridge the gap and be more realistic about life. I enjoy being married and it's good for me. It keeps me more solidly on the ground. He's a great help when I'm worried, or in pain, and sometimes he travels with me."

Erik Bruhn maintains that to be an artist one must be alone, but although some doubtless subscribe to that theory, many do not. "I never agreed with him on that," argued Miss Gregory. "I have told other people that I think he is lonely, although I have never said it to Erik. Maybe he wants to be alone, because he has stuck to that creed, but I love Erik and would love to be able to get closer to him. He feels that you shouldn't get married but think only of dance. I think he's wrong, but I suppose he's happy."

Children give an added dimension to many dancers' lives, and Ivan Nagy is among them. "Being married and having children is the best thing. I recommend them like a good recipe that I would like to pass on to everybody. I think having children and raising them is the greatest responsibility in the world. Marriage you share, but it's not the same. I did share with Marilyn [when there were only two of us] and I shall again, but it's not the same as having a family. You are responsible for [children's] every step. With the first child, it is especially difficult because you're learning how to be a father. For that you have to rely on your instinct and intelligence. There are no good books on the subject; what has been written is rubbish!"

Natalia Makarova is one of the few dancers in the West who has had a baby at the advanced stage of a career and then returned to performing. "Before having the baby I had only myself to think about. Now I have the baby and I worry about him, which is good. I wish I was with him more often, but to keep myself in shape all the time takes a lot of work. I only see him in the morning and after rehearsal, before he goes to sleep, which is not much."

After having a baby it is extremely difficult for a dancer to retrain her body back to the level required for performing. "Getting back into shape was very hard," continued Miss Makarova, "and that's true of dancers in general. You have to have enormous willpower. I had the ambition, not just to get back into shape, but to be better. It pushed me to work harder, be more conscientious, and more careful." When she appeared on stage again there was an added dimension to Miss Makarova's dancing. "Well, I have gained in having a son," Miss Makarova said, smiling. "So that is bound to affect me."

During a season, and in rehearsal periods, dancers usually have only one free day each week. At particularly hectic times, or in the event of an emergency, even that may be missed. Although, when missed, the day off may be rescheduled for another day when a dancer is not performing, and union requirements stipulate the minimum amount of free time dancers must be given, there are occasions when a dancer will forgo time off to cover a role in an emergency or to learn or rehearse a part he is hoping to be able to perform. A dancer's entire system is so full of energy when he is working that often during the weekly free day he is unable to relax. Only when the day comes to start a new week does he suddenly start to feel tired.

Dancers may have exciting, unusual, and even bizarre choices to make when offered jobs outside their own companies. They may be required to dress as animals to make television advertisements for an oil company, as happened to Peter Fonseca of American Ballet Theatre. Starr Danias was once offered the opportunity to dance a sensual pas de deux, *The Sacred Grove*, in Las Vegas for $10,000 a week for nine weeks. Starr mentioned the offer to Robert Joffrey in horror, thinking only of the performances she would miss while being away from his company. She recalls that Mr. Joffrey's eyes opened wide as he remarked, "Think of all the ballets we could stage." Starr was young at the time, and in retrospect believes that she was silly to turn down such an offer, considering how rarely such financial opportunities are offered to most dancers.

The artistic trait in dancers is frequently channeled into different art forms, some dance-related, others totally unconnected with it. Anthony Dowell's love for sketching and drawing resulted in his being invited to design costumes. "The first request was from Sir Frederic Ashton, when he created *The Dream*. He didn't want me to design the ballet, just do designs for some of the fairies, because he wanted ideas. Even though it was many years ago, I'm still really very pleased with them. They're quite good designs. I remember he wanted to keep them and I didn't want that to happen. Even then, I thought my ideas could be used. Years later, when he created the *Thaïs* pas de deux on Antoinette Sibley and me for a gala, Sir Fred asked me to design some costumes. He had established the colors he wanted and showed me different strands of wool. That was the first time my designs were used onstage."

Many creative talents are discovered through necessity. Lack of funds among some young dancers has promoted creativity that has grown into a second profession capable of providing an alternative means of support after a dancer retires. Bart Cook has become an expert at making stained-glass objects because, as a young dancer, he wanted a hobby to occupy him during sleepless nights. Once, when he and a group of roommates were moving into an apartment, they decided to furnish it from an auction gallery, as they needed to economize. While at the gallery, they saw some beautiful stained-glass windows, which could be used as a substitute for an apartment window through which there was a particularly uninteresting view. The window needed enlarging and Bart eventually planned to make a panel. After reading about the subject and consulting the Yellow Pages for stores, he proceeded. Now he makes jewelry boxes and lamps, and his stained-glass windows are commissioned by owners of fine houses and restaurants.

For a dancer who does not become a principal, it can be especially important that he find another outlet, both as a later means of financial support and as a boost to morale. Steven Caras told the eminent dance photographer Martha Swope of his interest in photography, and subsequently served as her apprentice. Ms. Swope, he says, is not only an invaluable teacher but a person who continues to show genuine interest in his success. "After more than eight years in ballet, I really became scared, because I was no longer eighteen [yet still in the corps] and wondered what I would do next. I didn't want to teach, because even though the training of future generations of dancers is important, I don't feel that's where my talent lies. Since I started photography, I have a certain inner calm, because I feel better about the future. It makes me happy to know there is something I can do other than dance, and the camera has added a marvelous dimension to my dance life."

Jimmy Dunne became a graduate of the Swedish Institute of Massage after studying with them for one year under the man Mr. Dunne names as the best masseur in the United States and Europe, Fred Kagan. During the year of study, Mr. Dunne gave up dancing to enable him to reevaluate his career. "Fred Kagan helped me both with my dancing and my future. I studied anatomy, so learned to understand injuries and their remedies. Consequently, when I started dancing again, I knew how to take care of myself. It became much easier to dance because the fear had gone. Pain and injuries can become very unnerving to dancers, especially when they don't understand the cause."

Rebecca Wright is interested in writing scenarios for ballets, and believes there is a genuine dearth of creativity nowadays. "Since sex and violence are so prevalent and available, there is nothing mysterious left, except God. . . . I think we need to return to fantasy, and the possibilities of using the mind. [People should not expect] to sit in the theatre and be titillated. The purpose of an art form is not only to entertain, but also to demand that the audience use their minds and work with the artists as it's happening. Otherwise, why not do something else? There is a lack of creativity in all art forms today, and when the conceivers lose that, then the arts are dying. In ballet, I think this is very true, although I shouldn't speak for modern dance. People are so bogged down with sensory experiences, they don't take time to sit down and think about the things that affect them in life, or to face each obstacle as it occurs. They avoid a certain responsibility toward their lives, and they cannot clearly create. There is too much confusion in their minds for them to be able to think out what is interesting, or where to place value in a work."

Most dancers' hobbies usually are artistic, and range from cookery to embroidery to fashion design. Athletic pastimes are few and far between, apart from swimming and perhaps the occasional game of tennis. There are two very practical reasons for this. To begin with, dancers have very little energy to devote to any pastime that is physically wearing. Also, just as a racehorse would not be expected to do the work of a carthorse, skiing, skating, athletics, etc., carry a high risk of injury to dancers. (Despite this fact, Fernando Bujones admits to having skied "just to see what it was like." He also confesses he would never risk it again while he is still dancing, and feels he is lucky to have come through unscathed. Ivan Nagy was always afraid to ski while still a dancer, feeling that for his sins he would be struck down with some terrible bodily injury.) Extensive walking is also generally avoided, as it works inappropriate muscles for dancers.

If dancers do not expect realistically to become stars or even to earn large sums of money, such thoughts probably sit pleasantly somewhere in their minds and sometimes come to the fore, maybe as they are walking home after a heady performance, mentally living life's imaginings.

"People ask me if I want to be a big star like Nureyev or Mischa, and I say no," claimed Peter Martins. "They don't have one thing in their lives that I would like. Of course, I would like to have a lot of money and a big villa, but I wouldn't give up anything I have for it. One thing I would like to have is a bodyguard around me whenever I want him there to do all the protective dirty work for me. Not that I'm being grabbed all the time, but I would like to have somebody to protect me from all the crazy, sick people in New York that I don't want to deal with. Rudi has a man with him all the time. He acts as a bodyguard and chauffeur and he takes care of everything, which leaves Rudi completely to his work. At first I was very turned off by the idea of it, because it looked very pretentious to me, but now I realize that it is not! Rudi has to put all of his energy into focus, and he can't be bothered with trivia. However, if I had a bodyguard, I would be laughed at [by the company]."

Mainly confined to their stables in a world that is so small, these human racehorses spend most of their time with their trainers and grooms. In the case of dancers totally devoted to either a company director or a choreographer whom they idolize, it is possibly not too far from the truth to say they are in the hands of their owners. Maybe a much admired choreographer is alternatively comparable with the jockey, being such a spiritual ally to the performer who is onstage, bringing his creativity to life. One thing is certain: Ballet dancers are a unique breed, set apart from the rest of humanity.

8

Dancers on Critics and a Critic on the Dance

O ye critics, will nothing melt ye?
—Sir Walter Scott's *Journal* (1825–32)

Sir Walter Scott's words remind us that critics have been around for a long time and that they, like the subjects they have been criticizing, have always been open to controversy.

Dancers, by virtue of their sensitivity, can be deeply affected by criticism. It is little comfort to an artist facing a negative review to be reminded that it is only one person's opinion, especially if the adverse criticism comes from one of the top critics.

The established critics basically serve as an eye-opener to the public, and the opinions of one who is informed can teach an individual what to look for and help him to recognize what he is seeing. When a critic offers his interpretation of a particular nuance he is supplying information to future generations of ballet historians. He is, in a sense, giving life to another side of a creation and hence adding a new dimension to it. The function of the dancer, choreographer, and all those who are related to a performance is to entertain and broaden the mind. The function of the critic is to record for current and future generations how far they succeeded.

Critics can sometimes become caught up in the politics of the dance world. "I think most critics start out by being straightforward and true to themselves," observed Peter Martins. "Then, gradually, they acquire a little more position, become more aware of where one company stands versus another, and begin to understand the intricacies of the ballet world. Then, suddenly you realize that the opinions they are giving are not their own."

Although criticism can have an adverse affect, it can also help to draw attention to dancers or companies who are trying to become established and who deserve support—or to the most famous dancers, who may be past their peak technically yet even more valid as performers through the artistry they have developed over the years. Kay Mazzo, a former principal with the New York City Ballet, feels the importance of keeping a sense of perspective. "It's always nice to have beautiful things said about you, but once it's over there's the next performance to think about, and you have to prove yourself all over again!"

Anthony Dowell reads reviews during a season. "One doesn't want to bury one's head in the sand. Sometimes it's good to be ready if people come up having read a critique and they pass comment. It's nice to know what they're talking about, but that goes in waves. Sometimes I just avoid reviews. At other times I feel compelled to get them. It becomes a mania. If you start with a good one, then you keep buying publications." He laughed. "Then when they start to go down a bit you lose interest in critiques. I honestly can't say that I've ever applied anything that's been said."

For a performer to be able to entertain and, even more, excite an audience, he must be secure in himself. A dancer is not only faced with the opinions of official critics, but also with those of colleagues, ballet masters, directors, choreographers, and friends. Martine van Hamel, like most dancers, learned the necessity for a dancer to remain objective about whom he trusts. "You have to be very careful how you interpret things, and to hold on to the one thing that's really important, which for me is dancing. You have to remain an individual and do things the way you feel are right for you. People will question you and offer all kinds of advice. As a dancer, you can succumb to that very quickly, and I've seen many people stumbling because they're searching; they're confused. They don't know why they're doing what they're doing. You can't dance if you hate everything, including—to some degree—dancing. After a while you think you hate that too."

Referring to the critics' reviews of her dancing, Miss van Hamel says she does not take much notice of what they say but adds that she is always complimented. "I don't know why. I've been lucky. It's easier to ignore something that's superlative. I think there's as much danger in receiving consistently good reviews as being subjected to too many that are negative. It's just more pleasant. Critics are not performing artists, they're writers. They don't know about dancing, simply writing. They only understand dance on one level. That's not to say that I think critics should be dancers. I don't think people have to have an intimate knowledge of dancing in order to understand it. I think it is much more important for critics to know about themselves than to know about dancing. They should at least have good taste. They need something much more elemental than knowing whether or not a step is hard [to execute]. The more involved you get in dancing and as a dancer, the harder it is to criticize and be objective about it. I'm not at all objective when I go to the ballet. I hate watching it for that reason. I can't separate myself from it."

Leading critics rarely give destructive rather than constructive critiques of the well-known dancers, which is only logical; as Clive Barnes stated in an interview, the reason a particular dancer is famous is because of his or her exceptional talent. Peter Martins said that if he gives a performance that is slightly under par, a critic usually will say that Mr. Martins had an off night.

Occasionally a famous dancer is panned, and Ivan Nagy suffered one such review in Washington. "It taught me never to read the critics during the season! Once when I was premiering *Cinderella,* a Washington critic came to a rehearsal. I was going through a very bad time generally—my father was seriously ill and a friend of mine had just died. I was not very happy. I was particularly aware of my complexes, and work was like a labor pain. As I walked into the studio, I happened to notice somebody I did not recognize and discovered upon inquiry that he was a critic. I then went to him and asked him very politely to leave the studio because of my frame of mind. When he asked why, I answered that it was because he was a critic. 'So,' he retorted. I apologized, but said that in the studio I felt I was entitled to my privacy. I told him that he could see me once the curtain went up, but while I was working in the studio I did not want him to see my agony. I explained that as I was sweating blood and exposing all my insecurities it was not good for him to see—after all, I was not invited to watch him writing a review! Should he find a marvelous word he had no idea how to spell, I was not there to see him look it up in the dictionary. I went on to say I found such things embarrassing, and asked that we should have mutual respect for privacy. As a result of this, the headline I received was that I was the most uncharming Prince Charming! I nearly died. I could not believe that he could have written such words, and it really hurt me. He went on about how rude and mannerless I was. He misunderstood me completely. I felt he should have limited himself to criticizing my dancing. It hurt me so badly that for three days I was in a state of mental collapse."

Added Miss Makarova, "Sometimes reviews are devastating to public opinion.

Everybody has a personal opinion, but I wish it were an independent, pure opinion. No one can be fully objective, because he is human. I think it's very dificult to be a critic, and certainly a very big responsibility."

On the subject of critiques, Anthony Dowell commented, "I think sometimes they can be destructive in that it's so tough being a dancer. You put so much of your heart into it that the knife really does go in when a performance is lightly written off. That attitude can be particularly hard if you hear positive comments from colleagues and the audience really got something from the performance. The printed word is very powerful." Dancers tend to place the most faith in the people with whom they work. "You can't see yourself dance, obviously, but one does trust certain colleagues in the company, and if they said your performance was wonderful, it is hard to take a bad review. In Chicago once, after a *Don Q.* [*Quixote*] I did with Gelsey [Kirkland] the critique was a humdinger, and quite untrue. Luckily, I am able to cope with such things now, but a few years ago it would have been very hard. I would have wondered why I bothered [to dance] at all."

Clive Barnes feels that, particularly in dance, critics on the whole develop a certain compassion when watching the performances of older dancers. A dancer's instrument is his body, and Mr. Barnes speculated as to what might happen if Yehudi Menuhin or Isaac Stern were to be handed a violin and warned that the instrument was going to deteriorate with every passing year. "A conductor at forty is a kid, but a dancer at forty is on his way out. A male dancer probably reaches his technical peak at about thirty-six to thirty-eight and a woman at about thirty-two. After that, there is a balance between artistry and ability." It is startling to reflect on how the performance of a great violinist would sound on a deteriorating instrument, or on the playing of Artur Rubinstein or Vladimir Horowitz on an eroding piano. Ivan Nagy retired at thirty-five, and of Clive Barnes's opinion on the stage at which he considers that men reach their peak, Mr. Nagy commented, "It's possible, but I think I reached my peak. It's hard to tell. Clive Barnes never performed in ballet shoes, so it's easy for him to say that from his position."

Mr. Barnes says that he has never known a dancer who learned from a critic. That is something he believes applies only to audiences. What he feels should be kept in mind is "the disturbing fact that ballet masters don't do their jobs," which causes dancers to look at the critic, unfairly, as a surrogate ballet master. However, if this is the case, why does a dancer not take notice of a critic's opinions and apply them? Maybe the difference between a dancer's preference to respect the criticisms of a colleague rather than those of a critic is that a colleague is, or has been, a dancer. Every time a dancer appears onstage, he runs the risk of not being on top of his performance. The mere anticipation of Aurora executing the "Rose Adagio" and the Bluebird going through the killing paces of his variations in *The Sleeping Beauty*, for example, can be moments of high suspense. The colleague who is still performing is all too aware of his own particular triumphs and less heroic moments on the stage. The artist who has stopped dancing to teach, choreograph, or become a ballet master recalls his dancing years. If he is working closely with a dancer in any of these capacities, he is to some extent responsible for that artist's performance. The dancer in part reflects his own expertise. The critic, on the other hand, is totally detached. He is in a position to speak more freely, and so is subjective—though bound, hopefully, by his conscience and sense of responsibility.

Sara Leland agrees that it is not the critic's function to correct dancers. The problem in the New York City Ballet, for example, she says, is that the company gives eight performances a week. Every studio at the State Theater is occupied daily until curtain time, and she feels an additional two studios would help to alleviate problems caused by lack of rehearsal space. In New York City alone, there is a three-month winter season and a two-month spring season. With the exception of December, which is devoted to *The Nutcracker*, most programs are composed of three or four different ballets from the repertoire. "People don't just walk around in dresses, either," she added ironically. "They dance." Last-minute injuries can cause great problems, especially when the corps is affected, and those dancers concerned must be gathered together to rehearse with the injured party's replacement.

Scott Barnard's reaction to Mr. Barnes's statement regarding ballet masters was that the comment was "absolutely outrageous." Any dancer has good and bad points. A ballet master teaches class in the mornings and rehearses performers all day, and will therefore be aware of any dancer's weak points, he added. Consequently, a ballet master does what he can to help that dancer. "A good ballet master will take a dancer who has been working on a role for a certain amount of time, before that dancer hits the stage with it. If the weak points are still showing through, then you either change the steps or maybe the angle. You may take a step and throw it away and accent the next one so that you camouflage the weak points as much as possible, until they become stronger points too. When a critic comes and watches a dancer, he is still going to see the weak points and he will comment on them. There is nothing that can be done about that. If a dancer does not have the legs and feet and natural strength in the ankles to jump, then he will never acquire that ability, but there are ways to make that jump look better, even if it means turning it into a throwaway step. You obviously won't emphasize it if it's going to look bad. In this way, a dancer looks the best that he can at any given moment."

The late entrepreneur Sol Hurok once told Mr. Barnes that he considered that the responsibility of the critic was to sell tickets. Mr. Barnes agreed with him, but qualified the statement by adding that the critic has a responsibility toward the audience and therefore has to decide which tickets he wants to sell. The critic does not teach the dancer how to dance, nor the choreographer how to choreograph, but should act as a bridge between the artist and audience, conveying to the latter what the dancer is trying to do. Of course, Mr. Barnes continued, this does not absolve the critic from judgmental evaluations. However, he believes he makes the subjectivity of his opinions very obvious—as he claims every critic should—leaving the reader or listener free to decide whether or not he concurs with a reviewer's evaluation.

It is possibly unfortunate that a ballet and its performers are reviewed by critics after only one performance. "A new ballet, or a dancer who's new to a role, really deserves more than one chance with the critics," claimed Jimmy Dunne. "When a dancer performs his first major role, or even solo, it is expected that he will perform well or he would not have been cast in it." A dancer in such a situation is under pressure because of what is expected of him. If he works well under pressure, this will be to his advantage. If he is unnerved by it, it can be his nemesis. Even though a respected critic is well qualified to judge ballets and their performers after one viewing, his opinions can change or at least be modified as he becomes more familiar with either one.

Bart Cook remembers being disappointed by one review. It occurred after a rumor had been spread that Mikhail Baryshnikov would be dancing in a performance for which Mr. Cook had been cast. Mr. Cook believes the rumor was spread by balletomanes who thought it would help to sell tickets. As the New York City Ballet has never sold tickets according to who is dancing, but rather on what is being danced, ultimately nobody benefited. A critic, obviously having expected to see Mr. Baryshnikov, said that Mr. Cook had been good in the performance, but that he was not Mikhail Baryshnikov. He did speak out, also, against the spreading of rumors, but the critique became another aspect of the damage done on all sides. The ballet in which Mr. Cook appeared on that occasion was *Rubies*, one of the three sections of Mr. Balanchine's work *Jewels*. Mr. Cook partnered Heather Watts in the performance, which apparently went well and was appreciated by the audience. To add to the irony, when critics watch a performance to which they go expecting Mr. Cook to dance, they almost invariably give him complimentary reviews. Added Mr. Cook, "Critics, I suppose, can do much to demoralize a dancer, but the dancer should know instinctively whether or not criticism is appropriate. Whoever is entitled to tell dancers what to do, it certainly should not be critics. It is only necessary to be sensitive to each ballet's creator, and the choreographer will let you know soon enough whether or not you're achieving that!"

Once any critic has seen a particular ballet and certain dancers in the same roles a sufficient number of times, the problem of keeping a review fresh would seem to be difficult. "*Swan Lake* I must have seen very close to a thousand times," speculated Mr. Barnes. "When you think that every *Swan Lake* lasts three hours, that is quite a formidable segment of my waking life watching that particular ballet. Now, would I have done that for *Hamlet*? No, I would not. I think that dance critics and audiences hold 'watching brief' on a performance. You can tune in and tune out in ballet, but it is much more difficult to do that in drama. I find also that there is much more variation, in a curious way, in dance than drama. Drama is much more stratified. I don't mean that in any bad sense. I really mean that an actor finds a portrayal that he offers as his, and sometimes he varies scarcely at all. Actors I have noticed in many performances of the same role— Olivier or Gielgud, for example—changing very little. Dancers change a great deal. I suppose the dancer I've seen most over the years is Fonteyn, and Margot has changed; she's developed. She changes from performance to performance. It's quite extraordinary. You would never find that in an actor or actress."

The question has frequently been raised as to whether art should be subjected to criticism. Ultimately, all that matters is that the performers and those who go to watch them enjoy themselves. If audiences go with the intention of liking a ballet, they should find some pleasure in it, even if it is only in the knowledge of the years of training and constant daily exertion that are required of the performers to even be on the stage—not forgetting the other people who choreograph for them or who work in other capacities to keep them there.

At the end of a performance given by the Royal Ballet at the Metropolitan Opera House, Swiss artist Martine Dupont, transfixed, continued staring at the stage as the curtain fell. Her mind still experiencing the ballet, she declared. "Dance is a way of reaching God. When these artists perform they are living in another dimension which common people cannot reach. At the moment of dancing, they are immortal." Since time immemorial, dance has been used as a form of worship. Maybe that is the reason.

9

Injuries and Physical Condition

$\mathcal{D}$ancers, like all athletes, are highly susceptible to injury. They are as in tune with their bodies as any musician is with his instrument, and as aware when it is "off key." From experience they can become very proficient at diagnosing what is wrong when they feel pain, and will frequently be able to gauge whether a particular injury can be worked through or needs some form of attention. The principal types of treatment that dancers require are orthopedics, podiatry, chiropractic, osteopathy, massage, shiatsu, and acupuncture. Administrators of these methods are now becoming more willing than they previously were to accept one another's practices because a treatment that is highly effective on one dancer can sometimes be of no appreciable benefit to another. The treatment a dancer believes will help him is most frequently the one that will solve his problem, provided he is selective about the type of doctor.

Dr. William G. Hamilton is an orthopedist who ministers to many dancers. He is the official consultant to the New York City Ballet and also treats many members of American Ballet Theatre and the Joffrey Ballet. There are two major types of injuries to dancers, Dr. Hamilton says, one being the acute, traumatic injury, of which the most common is the sprained ankle. Other such injuries are broken wrists, usually caused by falling; damage to shoulders, torn knee cartilages, etc. These can be caused by a drop from a lift or rough placement to the floor that may cause a foot to catch. The second category, which Dr. Hamilton maintains probably incorporates the greater number of injuries, is called the "overuse syndrome." Dancers frequently develop tendinitis and stress fractures, he says, "from just pounding away" at their bodies. "The New York City Ballet has almost a hundred dancers, and . . . there are often as many as fifteen or twenty of them out with injuries at any one time. Although the injuries to some may be minor, everybody is currently very hung-up on the fact that they're dancing in pain—and they are! It is difficult to encourage them to stop dancing with minor injuries, but if they're really hurting top professionals would rather not appear onstage at all than dance poorly."

Although all athletes suffer to some extent from injuries, Dr. Peter Bullough, orthopedic pathologist at the Hospital for Special Surgery in New York, believes that dancers may suffer the least per man-hour of exercise because their movements are the most controlled. A tremendous amount of effort is put into obtaining ultimate stretch, he says, and when they are working properly in a controlled way, dancers should not injure themselves. Dr. Bullough maintains also that the more experienced a dancer, the less likely the risk of injury, and that physical problems are not simply proportional to the amount a particular dancer works. The more practiced the dancer, the more accurately he will probably work his body, claims Dr. Bullough, and the more awareness he will have of its weaknesses and shortcomings. This, he feels, is the fundamental difference between ballet and "the other contact sports," because the better the footballer, the more aggressive he will be. The more risks he takes, the greater will probably be the number of injuries suffered. The man who protects himself and does not push forward is probably not a very good footballer.

Both hard stages and switching styles in a performance can cause injuries to dancers. Going from the classical or neoclassical to modern style, or vice versa, requires changes in technique and in areas of the body that must take strain. The former emphasizes the long, stretched-out line and the latter involves contractions and such feats as knee turns, which, though they may be choreographically effective, can be damaging to the knee joint.

Dancers sometimes have difficulty differentiating between serious and inconsequential pain. Says Dr. Hamilton, "An injury that is potentially serious can masquerade early on as being ordinary. The classic example is the shin splint. If dancers suffer pain in their shins, they believe it to be a shin splint and they'll continue to work. After about nine months they come to me and find that it's not a shin splint at all but three or four fractures in the bone. That is a stress fracture. Often I can't even tell the difference without an X ray, which I have to examine very closely. Sometimes fatigue fractures don't show up on an initial X ray, but only two or three weeks later, once they have begun to heal." Dr. Bullough elaborated: "The bone is made up of little rods, especially at the ends. Everybody regularly breaks these little struts of bone—it can happen when running after a bus. These heal up and don't give any problem, but if they are acquired at a very rapid rate, then it is possible for a fatigue break to occur in the bone. Dancers and hikers, for instance, are particularly susceptible because of the prolonged unusual exercise they take."

Dr. Bullough remarked on the degree of pain tolerance among dancers, who have been known to dance on broken toes, for example. A jogger would rarely consider running under such circumstances, but when a dancer is involved in his art, although he may experience pain at first, he will eventually become preoccupied with dancing and will cease to be aware of pain. That can be a disadvantage to a dancer because, Dr. Bullough continued, pain indicates a problem and is the signal to stop using the area that hurts. If that message is deliberately avoided, then an injury may become serious.

Dr. Hamilton believes that a dancer's level of pain endurance is partly psychological and partly the self-discipline that is learned from the outset of training. However, he thinks that the ability to dance with an injury and feel little or no pain to some extent must be physiologically related. "They are so keyed up—the adrenaline is pumping—and the pain becomes insignificant."

Most men are not as tolerant of pain and not as courageous as women, maintains chiropractor Dr. Rose Smart. Men, she said, have more of a tendency to panic over injuries because they do not comprehend the body as well as women do. This, she believes, is principally because women are built for childbearing, which is accompanied by so much pain. Dancers, in general, said Dr. Smart, have a better pain tolerance than most other people because of their greater body awareness. A layman tends to be nervous and then pain becomes more acute. Dancer Sallie Wilson bears out the theory of pain tolerance in her statement, "I was brought up to believe that if you can crawl, you keep going."

One of the dancer's principal deterrents against injury is a body that is warmed up slowly and sufficiently for the strain his art form demands. Physiologically, this increases the flow of blood to the muscles, stated Dr. Hamilton, and stretches out the tightness in the muscles and tendons. It loosens up the body. Professional dancers' major enemy is tightness, not weakness, he maintains. Strength they will acquire usually from working. Occasionally they will have some unrecognized weakness that does predispose danger, "and that's where I think my work is very important. I can sometimes pick up on a weakness or defect in technique that is causing a recurrent difficulty or pattern of injury. The treatment of dancers has two phases; one is to cure the injury, the second is to find its cause. That is most important, as frequently it is the only way of preventing its reoccurrence. Often when a dancer pulls a hamstring, for example, he'll admit he didn't warm up before a rehearsal, or that he warmed up, rehearsed, and then sat around for an hour or so before going back into rehearsal not properly warmed up."

Many people incorrectly believe that as they warm up the body and stretch out the muscles, they are also stretching out the ligaments and tendons, said Dr. Bullough, although the amount of stretch in these is only about one or two percent.

Professional dance as a Darwinesque phenomenon constantly impresses Dr. Hamilton. The system weeds out those with poor training, the wrong body type, etc., from the time they start training as children. Those who enter any of the world's leading companies have great natural ability, combined with the other attributes required to succeed in dance.

A study has now been done on the development of the hip joint, stated Dr. Hamilton, though it was not confined to dancers. What a dancer refers to as "turnout" is known as retroversion of the hip. Dr. Hamilton confirmed that results have shown this will change very little after the age of eight or nine (before which time a child should not be given ballet training). The soft tissue around the joints can be stretched, but if a child is basically pigeontoed he will never acquire good turnout. If he is encouraged to force it he will develop serious trouble somewhere between the ages of thirteen and fifteen. Troubles usually happen at the knee, said Dr. Hamilton, because that takes most of the strain. When the foot is trying to turn out and the hip's natural tendency is to turn in, the result is frequently a dislocated kneecap, which, Dr. Hamilton added, "is simply mother nature trying to tell a student he is wrong for ballet." Dr. Bullough talked of movement in the hip joint, which he said is very limited in extension and external rotation. "The ligaments around the hip are formed in a screw distribution and when the hip is turned out it becomes progressively tighter, especially if the leg is extended as it is being pushed back. It can be turned in a great deal more than turned out. Dancers are always trying to improve their turnout, and the only way to do that is to pull the ligaments apart. A ligament looks like a rope made of numerous fibers, and, as it is unstretchable, the only way to lengthen it is by causing minute tears." Although it can heal, the place where it is torn remains slightly apart, states Dr. Bullough. A dancer who trains his body from childhood will gradually develop artificial laxity, but should he stop dancing, or at least taking class, the body will tend to go back to its original state.

One of the most common injuries suffered by dancers is a "knot" in a muscle, which Dr. Hamilton explained is the result of that muscle being pulled. When muscle fibers are strained or pulled apart, there is a degree of local hemorrhage in the muscle. The amount of bleeding will vary, but the blood that escapes from the vessels is very irritating to the body. Bleeding into a muscle can cause it to cramp initially, and to "knot." Later a "knot" may become permanent or semi-permanent, because the bleeding into the tissue eventually causes some scar tissue to form.)Scar tissue is inelastic compared to the elasticity of the local muscle tissue, says Dr. Hamilton. Often there will be a little wad of scar tissue left in the muscle where it was pulled, but ultimately a pulled muscle can recover as scar tissue is remolded and stretched out again. Healing is usually achieved either through massage of a "knot," applied exercise, or a combination of the two.

Dancers generally will maintain muscle tone while they continue to work, as muscles used daily rarely soften in the age range within which most dancers are active.

The predominant injuries vary between companies, depending to a large extent on the choreography. Sprains and tendinitis are very common to the Balanchine style because of the rapid movement, close timing, etc., claims Dr. Hamilton. At American Ballet Theatre, especially among the men, the emphasis on jumping tends to produce stress fractures, bruised heels, and jarred ankles.

Although tendinitis is a common injury among dancers, particularly in the Achilles tendon, only rarely does a tendon snap, sometimes ending a dancer's career, stated Dr. Hamilton. (Two cases were Brian Shaw, a principal with the Royal Ballet, while dancing the Bluebird during a performance of *The Sleeping Beauty*—Anthony Dowell, dancing Prince Florimund on that occasion, substituted for him—and Nels Jorgensen of the Joffrey Ballet, whose career onstage ended with that company.) A partial rupture is often treated in plaster, and this occurs when the Achilles tendon is damaged but the tear is incomplete. Some patients with acute, total ruptures are treated in plaster, but the evidence shows that for a professional athlete the Achilles tendon will not heal up strongly enough to be functional. At one time a ruptured Achilles tendon meant a dancer would never be able to return to the stage, but nowadays, if an operation is performed competently and early, the continuation of a performing career is possible. Dr. Hamilton has treated two or three such cases. The Achilles tendon does not rupture cleanly, he affirms, but shreds, and repairing it is like trying to sew the ends of two paintbrushes together. "The ends just sit there flopping in the breeze. In the past they were bunched together and allowed to heal. Although it worked effectively, the tendon was also shorter, and with a dancer it must be restored to its original length. If it is too short, he can't plier, and if on the long side, it is impossible to relever. The operation is extremely complicated and must be done by somebody who understands dancers, but unfortunately, there are not many such surgeons around. Very few see a sufficient number of dancers to enable them to build up their expertise, and there is very little medical literature available on the subject. Fortunately, now that dancing is becoming more popular, the knowledge is growing."

Dr. Bullough explained that when the Achilles tendon snaps, a person feels as if he has been given a firm kick in the heel, which is usually accompanied by a loud crack. "It is extremely uncomfortable, and usually happens as the result of some unaccustomed or exaggerated movement."

Dr. Rose Smart treats a great many dancers who, in her experience, know from the way the body feels when it is time for either medical treatment or massage. Dancers who find chiropractic beneficial usually will visit her daily initially, especially if they need to perform, and she has kept patients onstage by ministering to them before a performance and afterward to undo the damage that has occurred in the interim. "I have improvised equipment at home for dealing with emergencies, and there was a time when I made arrangements with a particular ballerina to visit me wherever I was after a performance," reminisced Dr. Smart. "The incident happened maybe ten years ago and she had waited a lifetime to do a certain role. Because of this lady's injury, it was necessary that I have her on her back and that she flex her legs against me. I would then give her a push, and the force of my body against her would put the lumbar back in place. I was less aware of the strength of a dancer then. She looked so frail, and I thought to myself that I would have to be careful how much weight I put on her. I then told her to push with all her might. She did, and I had to peel myself off the wall! More recently, I did that with a male dancer and he broke one of my ribs. I've stopped that method now."

Dr. Smart emphasized that she does not like to treat a patient so frequently and knows rest would be better than performing under such circumstances. However, she feels a dancer who has waited many years to dance a part could suffer psychologically in a way that would be even more traumatic. Once crucial performances are over, Dr. Smart recommends that a dancer rest for as long as possible and receive the necessary amount of adjustment. If the muscles and ligaments that hold the skeleton together are injured, either by being torn or by losing their tone, it is analogous to an overstretched rubber band, stated Dr. Smart. Until the tone is rejuvenated, the affected parts of the skeletal structure will not hold in place.

Most doctors who minister to dancers are accustomed to the occasional request for treatment of an injury that will make performing possible. "If a dancer wants to do a part very badly for a particular reason, then I have to sit down and do a little soul-searching," declared Dr. Hamilton. "I have to consider whether or not a dancer is going to do permanent damage to herself if she decides to perform in spite of pain. If she is willing to put up with that, usually she can appear onstage. Sometimes there are things that can be done, like strapping or taping the ankles. I may also recommend aspirin or something mild that will take the edge off the pain; then, if a dancer warms up well and puts ice on an injury after a performance, she should be all right. What I will never do is inject somebody with Novocaine or give them very strong pain medicine and send them onto the stage."

As with Dr. Smart, Dr. Hamilton will help a dancer perform with an injury only if the chances of serious damage are unlikely. He does emphasize that healing will be delayed for a week or two, and makes sure that a dancer fully understands the course of action he or she is taking. "Fortunately, I've been around dancers long enough now that they do have confidence in my judgment, which they did not have at first. They would go and see six or eight doctors until finally they would often find one who would give them the answer they were looking for and they would stick with him. I've always tried to be open and honest and not dogmatic. If a dancer insists on dancing with a fracture, yet claims she can't even go up on pointe, I then ask her how she thinks she will be able to perform. Usually, at that stage she will take my advice and rest until the injury is healed."

Certain doctors and dancers believe in the use of cortisone to combat injury. Dr. Bullough spoke of its negative effects. "Cortisone injections are applied to joints, tendons, muscles, etc., but cortisone is a two-edged sword. Cortisone will reduce the inflammation—but remember that inflammation is the first step toward healing. Some people believe that inflammation occurs only with infections. But that is not so; it occurs after all injuries. If that initial reaction is suppressed, then so is the entire healing process. At first an injury becomes slightly swollen, red, and painful. Cortisone greatly reduces pain and swelling, which is the indication to rest the part. So as both the warning and the healing are being suppressed, only the pain will go away, but the injury could become worse as a result of the insensitivity. . . . You can produce extremely severe arthritic changes with sufficient cortisone, and this may be iatrogenically produced. Dancers who develop severe arthritis in old age may be in pain because of all the cortisone shots, or pushing themselves too hard and dancing when they should not have. The problem is, they don't pay the price the next day; they pay it ten or twenty years later."

For eleven years Merle Park suffered from an injury that she considered to be an occupational hazard that either would heal or was worsening arthritis. She believes it probably started in childhood, when she was continuously catching her feet in the spokes of a bicycle while being carried on the back of it. After eleven years of dancing with the injury while it grew progressively worse, Miss Park finally found the pain excessive. "I could hardly get my foot off the ground. It was agony—it simply wouldn't stretch out. I went to see a marvelous Danish doctor who said that he would operate and that the problem could be corrected. The operation was amazing. He lifted the Achilles [tendon] and had to scrape away all the cortisone that had been pumped into me and had completely stuck to the bursa and the bone. He then had to chisel the bone down almost to the marrow, wax it, lay the Achilles back, and stitch me up." As there was nothing wrong with the Achilles tendon, and cutting it would only have created further problems, the doctor used his skill to ensure that it remained intact. The readjustment to being able to use her foot normally took many months, after which time Miss Park was able to dance her most demanding roles once more, including Aurora in *The Sleeping Beauty*. Miss Park felt the operation had been highly successful, as prior to it even walking had been painful.

Today's technical demands and busy schedules take their tolls in terms of injuries, and masseur Robert Legrand, who ministers to many of the world's leading dancers, spoke of the dangers. A dancer, he said, must concentrate fully on what he is doing. When he plays the prince, clown, or other role, he must go out of character to do the tricks. "They cannot be done with a smile. Dancers should watch circus people and the very dangerous tricks they do, because if they're wrong, they get killed. At one time, no dancer would have dreamed of doing what Gelsey Kirkland can do with her body today, or would even have believed such feats to be possible. The jumps that Baryshnikov can do are amazing. If he made a wrong move, he could break a leg." A tremendous amount of time must be devoted to the art of jumping and landing, and when they land dancers must have adequate spring in their legs. The heels, knees, and hips should each take some of the shock, so that it is evenly distributed. To some extent this is instinctive, but it should be continuously pointed out to people in class, from childhood on, emphasized Dr. Bullough.

The Cecchetti style of ballet is designed to accommodate the architecture of the body more than any other, stated Dr. Smart. "I don't think he realized the need for what he was doing—he was doing it for beauty—but it happens to be the case." She believes that one of the reasons the style is so attractive is that it is not laborious by balletic standards.

Arthritis is a principal problem from which dancers can suffer, and the feet and hips are two areas that are frequently affected. "This is hardly surprising, since ballet puts such a strain on these two areas," claimed Dr. Bullough. For the women, dancing on their toes puts a tremendous strain on the foot, and the extension and ranges of movement required by both women and men make unreasonable demands on the hips.

Dr. Bullough remarked on the speed with which dancers tend to recover from injuries, even after operations, as compared to the average person, but this, he maintains, is because of their superior physical condition. Joints, he said, especially the knee, are protected by the muscles on either side. The better developed the calf and thigh, the more protection the knee has. As dancers have such well-developed legs, their knees are protected to a certain extent, stated Dr. Bullough, which enables them to make quick recoveries.

Ivan Nagy once recuperated from an injury with a rapidity that startled his doctors. "Believe it or not, I have an extra vertebra," said Mr. Nagy. "Maybe I'll end up in the Natural History Museum!" When he was about thirty, he slipped a disk during a performance of *Paquita*. "I finished the pas de deux, despite the lifts and the injury. Somehow, you have such incredible willpower, you don't want to give out in front of the audience. I did a lift on one hand and threw my partner up in the air, and as she came down I caught her. Just at that moment there was a terrible noise and I knew that my disk had gone out. We still had so many different steps to do. As we danced, I kept looking at the wings, hoping I would make it. I could not take a bow after it was over. Once the music finished I went stiff. So, with dignity, and feeling very tense, I just walked off the stage. Then I collapsed, paralyzed. It was awful. Fortunately, I had immediate help from the right people, but it was all most unpleasant. I was in heavy stage makeup, sweaty and in costume and they took me to the hospital for an X ray in that state. Then I was informed I had a slipped disk, as if I didn't know! In came a huge, most unpleasant nurse, and I was moved without any feeling for the fact that I was in absolute agony. It was painful even to talk. To make matters worse, she was extremely slanderous and I was not in a position to defend myself. She took my clothes off in such a heavy-handed way that my back went back [into place]. Severe muscle spasms followed, because the tissues were really damaged. The pain was excruciating. The doctor told me that I should not dance for three months, which I emphasized to him meant six months without working, as I would need an additional three months to get my strength back to perform again. He didn't really understand, but I reminded him of the brevity of a dancer's career. I then took shiatsu and acupuncture treatments, and was back on stage one week after the injury. Nobody could believe it."

Extreme temperature changes are unhealthy for anyone, but can be extremely hazardous to dancers. When the temperature is ninety or one hundred degrees and a dancer is very lightly dressed after taking class, he may walk into a building where the air is twenty or thirty degrees cooler. The draft, says Mr. Legrand, can cause the neck and back to go into spasms, and consequently he gives as many massages in the summer as at any time of the year. Dancers have to battle also against air conditioning in a theatre. "The air conditioning that flows across a stage is enough to freeze them to death, and it is especially bad if they have to stand out there during *Giselle, Swan Lake,* or other ballets of this nature. You can feel the muscles go together like pieces of ice. Then they have to dance."

Some ballet companies have an official masseur who, in certain cases, travels with them. Mr. Legrand feels that it is impossible to be right for everybody when working with fifty to a hundred people. "I think it is necessary to be in tune with a person to be able to help them to the fullest extent. Technically I do the same things, but you disturb a person's psyche when you give them a good massage. I'm not simply referring to the degree of pain. You make tremendous contact. An hour's massage of the type that I give is worth far more than an hour's lovemaking, because people don't handle each other that way. You don't feel like you've been plummeted to the depths on almost every part of your body. It's a highly erotic business. There's a very deep psychic disturbance. If you believe in the psychic world, you recognize that you're very much in touch with the astral soul—totally under the aura. Many dancers are clairvoyant, and some of them are very powerful psychics. There are people I can just run my hand over and feel a certain electricity."

A proficient masseur or doctor also is part psychologist. Occasionally a dancer will go to Mr. Legrand with a problem that is more emotional than physical, and principally requires a sympathetic ear. Only rarely is there disturbance of a nature that causes Mr. Legrand to suggest that a dancer seek psychiatric help. Lack of promotion, or fewer roles than a dancer thinks he should have, can cause him to pour out his feelings verbally as he is being massaged. It is all caused by the politics and learning to play the game in the large ballet companies, claims Mr. Legrand. "It happens less in modern dance because the companies aren't so large. Studies have shown that a supervisor can't deal effectively with more than fifteen people. Now that ballet companies are so large, they are dealing with stresses that never existed before. This is yet another reason why masseurs who treat dancers are so busy nowadays, as well as the longer seasons, higher technical demands, etc. There was a time when dancers only worked for about six months of the year. Often they went on horrendous one-night-stand tours, but they gave the same performance night after night, so that they hardly ever got hurt. Given the enormous pressures dancers are under today, a reaction can start in the mind and sometimes the body creates an injury to let the body rest. When it can't take any more, the weak spot gives way.''

Body type basically dictates the frequency with which a dancer goes for a massage. Dancers are all different muscularly, and their metabolisms, genetic makeup, and bone structures vary, stated Mr. Legrand. Consequently, he said, there are many dancers who have never had a massage, while others go every week. "One person can have muscles that are as pliable as a wet sponge and the next one gives you the impression you're working on a Michelangelo statue— marble. They just won't budge; you can't make a dent in the flesh. That means a very painful massage, but you get the circulation going. Those who have the hard muscles have to come in for treatment, not because of the exercise but the body type." In Mr. Legrand's experience, problems fall into two main areas, the lower back and the calves. Also, some have trouble with hips and there are a number of small bone deformities that exist, he said. Those with bone deformities go for massage the most frequently, to compensate for them. "Many people in this country were put into ballet because pediatricians discovered they had a curvature of the spine, or maybe were either knockkneed or bowlegged or their feet were weak. Once the mother had put the child into ballet class, if the talent was there that child ended up as a dancer." Maybe it is in spite of certain physical problems, and a determination to prove that they were not a deterrent, that many dancers are onstage today.

Some people cannot take a massage because their nervous system is overly sensitive for it and the pressure hurts too much, claims Mr. Legrand. If dancers have abused their bodies sufficiently, only rest will heal them unless they want to endure the pain of massage. He added that it can be difficult to impress on people that a correctly given massage is painful only when something is wrong with the body, because a healthy body can withstand a tremendous amount of pressure. "Somebody who has been through pain in many sessions will finally stop suffering. Then they ask if I'm pressing as hard as before and I tell them that if I went any harder I'd be through the table. It is simply that the muscles are no longer giving resistance and I can move the blood. Then it feels good and they are convinced."

Massage enables Mr. Legrand to feel deeply enough into the body to diagnose many problems that require the attention of either a doctor or a chiropractor, at which time he recommends the treatment he thinks would better serve the dancer concerned.

A massage lasts one hour for Mr. Legrand's patients, during which time he works on both sides of the body, treating the legs, arms, back, and back of the neck. However, if a dancer has a specific injury Mr. Legrand may apply the entire hour to it. He must judge also how long he can work on a given ailment, because overworking an area, he says, can cause bruises.

The oldest form of medicine is possibly massage, based on the premise that if some part of the body becomes painful the basic instinct is to rub it. Mr. Legrand occasionally uses a heat lamp or ultrasound treatment. The heat helps to move the blood, bringing nutrients at a greater rate to certain injuries, he says, and the ultrasound sends high-frequency waves into tissue. "Ultrasound is used only on very limited areas," emphasized Mr. Legrand. "You don't run it over a person like a vibrator, or use it often on the same individual, because it can be destructive. It vibrates the molecular structure of the muscle and you can break down scar tissue with it. Sometimes damage [to a muscle] is so bad, the scar tissue feels like a steel band in the muscle. I sometimes also use ultrasound on a badly knotted muscle and Achilles tendon problems, as well as around the ankle, and on the ligaments around the knee. The application is very short—only about three or four minutes. The results can be amazing, and muscle goes from having that steellike consistency to being soft and pliable. Scar tissue has to be broken down in one of two ways—either through physical activity or ultrasound."

Mr. Legrand does not like to give a full massage to a person under eighteen, and limits treatments to areas such as the ankle in these cases. The protective myelin sheath that surrounds the fibers of certain nerves is not completely formed before about that age, he says, and consequently young people are very sensitive to pain and pressure.

The back has been a weak area in man ever since he first became a biped, and it is not uncommon for people to injure that area by a sudden movement, for example. Back injuries are prevalent among male dancers mainly as the result of lifting the women during partnering. The women are underweight by the standards of the general populace, claims Mr. Legrand, but many of them are tall. He maintains that ideally, there should be a differential of 30 pounds between a man and a woman, yet claims that some boys weigh only about 125 pounds and that there are very few girls who weigh less than 100 pounds. The majority probably are closer to 110 pounds. If a lift could be done always with perfect control, back injuries would probably be considerably reduced, but because there is movement involved, and lifts are made from many different angles, a man's back takes an inordinate amount of strain. Ideally, he should be able to keep his spine erect, and be able to bend his legs so that basically they take the strain. However, today, due to the technical capabilities of ballet dancers, audiences expect to see superhuman feats performed with apparently no effort. Jirí Kylián, artistic director of the Netherlands Dance Theatre, and that company's principal choreographer, has choreographed a ballet entitled *Symphony in D*. It is a cleverly orchestrated spoof on classical ballet that, interestingly, serves a double purpose. While its humor stems from showing what could go wrong in ballet if it were in the hands of those less than expert, especially in partnering, it also puts emphasis on the necessity for expertise. Anything less and classical ballet can be dangerous and also a mockery, because of its highly structured patterns of movement.

Daniel Duell, New York City Ballet principal, has several times been hospitalized and put in traction because of back trouble. He maintains that men hurt their backs because they are never taught basic weight-lifting principles. In partnering classes, he says, there is very little education on the mechanical process of lifting, and that which exists is unstructured. Points that are necessary to remember for the long-term health of the back are not sufficiently emphasized. Although it is possible to keep the back straight and take the weight in the legs when lifting, "it's hard to remember to do that all the time with every lift in every direction. Sometimes you're supporting a lift for a long time, and high lifts are not so much of a problem as low lifts. Back problems are inevitable to some degree, but I think they could be alleviated somewhat if weight lifting was an integral part of dance training. So much depends on the partner, and also the ballet itself. There are occasions when a girl's total body weight must be lifted without any help from her, because it is choreographed that way. That means you're lifting dead weight. Also, there are girls who, when you lift them, feel like they're trying to get back on the ground!" Said Jimmy Dunne, "The problem is that during the performance you will do anything you have to to make a step work. If you're in the wrong position you will strain every muscle in your body if necessary to achieve something, instead of giving in as you would in rehearsal. In that case, if you're doing a lift and something doesn't feel quite comfortable, you stop the proceedings and start again, in order not to hurt yourself. Onstage you can't do that."

Many dancers these days, both men and women, take regular exercises as a deterrent against injuries, in institutions that provide equipment designed to build strength and stamina. Bart Cook, an implicit believer in this form of exercise, says he has strengthened the weak parts of his body by using equipment and has learned how to use one muscle as opposed to another. "It makes muscle tone and has changed the shape of my body. My rear end has pulled up and my waistline is higher because of the different shape of the muscle."

At one time girls generally suffered more from the fear of growing too tall than of being too short, but today, in the New York City Ballet, and to an increasing extent at American Ballet Theatre, this is no longer the case. Five foot seven is a popular height. Martine van Hamel recalls having dreaded becoming too tall for ballet. She thinks that maybe it was all the energy that went into dancing, together with sheer determination, that held down her growth. "It was a very big issue when I was younger. I was really considering drinking gin! It is only since I started to dance professionally that dancers have got taller."

The amount of energy a dancer's body must produce to make any given movement varies with his size. Said Mr. Legrand, "It's much harder for Peter Martins to move his body around than it is for Mikhail Baryshnikov. If you read elementary physics on rocketry, you learn the difference between what it takes to get a hundred pound load off the ground and what it takes to move two hundred pounds. If you double the weight, it takes considerably more than twice the amount of energy. Peter Martins probably weighs around one seventy-five and Baryshnikov about one thirty-five. That forty-pound difference takes a good deal more energy to thrust into the air." (The difference in the two men's height is about eight inches.)

Natalia Makarova has one of the smallest bone structures imaginable. "Her bones are tiny and she has the most beautiful muscles," stated Mr. Legrand. "Yet she's very strong and has such a remarkable sense of her body that she rarely gets hurt. The boys say partnering her is like having a baton in their hands. She knows exactly how to place her weight. It takes no effort to dance with her."

Mr. Legrand has concluded that a typical feature of almost every famous ballerina is that she has big feet in proportion to her body size. If they have small feet, he said, they have insufficient stability. "Long, narrow feet also present problems for dancers, and they are more likely to suffer from shin splints, tendinitis, hip and back problems, because the base is not strong. You need a good, wide peasant foot at the end of those beautiful legs! The size of the foot in relation to the body is what gives them that firm base to stand on, even on pointe."

Jimmy Dunne said that it is an advantage for a dancer not to have an ideal body because he must work harder, which consequently will build his strength. "You have to develop an understanding of what you are doing, in a way that those who are able to do things naturally do not. They do everything correctly and don't know what it feels like to be off balance. If the situation were the same in the U.S. as it is in Russia [where a good ballet body is mandatory], that would eliminate a great many of the dancers that we have, because very few of them are ideally built for ballet."

Chiropractic, which has been a salvation for many dancers, is based on neurophysiology and body balance, Dr. Smart confirmed. The body is divided into two halves, left and right. If there is displacement of one or the other half, there is unequal pull on the muscles, which renders a dancer more prone to injury than he would be were the skeleton correctly balanced. "Some dancers have been made posture-conscious at all times," stated Dr. Smart. "Sallie Wilson and Gelsey Kirkland, for example, have the most perfect spines. They have perfect alignment. If a body is not well balanced, and the pelvis not square, you can't use one leg as freely as the other. If you're unaware of body balance and force it to make it work, it will eventually collapse." When a curvature of the spine develops, it can often cause a knee injury, said Dr. Smart. "If you go to a medical doctor, they will probably confine themselves to the knee. I concern myself with the pelvic region. If that is all right, then the knee will be, because the muscles in the pelvic region are headed for the knee. The knee, being the most distant point from origin, is the first to go." The most common injuries that Dr. Smart treats, she said, are those in the lower back, a dislocated femur head, or the knee, ankle, or foot.

Dancers, being artists, generally are open to new ideas. Consequently, for treatment of injuries many have turned to the ancient Chinese science of acupuncture, a practice that in some Western eyes still is regarded with suspicion because of its recent advent here. Acupuncturist Dr. George Hsu said the object of acupuncture is to restore and maintain normal circulation and to keep the nervous system in tone. This, he added, is beneficial to the general health. He claims also that it can keep the digestive system in good order, which consequently improves the complexion and makes a patient look younger. "A person who has both good nervous and digestive systems," concluded Dr. Hsu, "has nothing to fear!"

Merrill Ashley finds acupuncture very effective. "It heals. I've had many injuries that it's helped with. Sometimes when my calves are tight, which is frequently, it can be very beneficial. It depends on where the needles go in as to whether or not you feel them. Some of them don't hurt at all. All I feel is a little pinprick. The needles are left in for about fifteen minutes, and once they're in they generally don't hurt. Its just miraculous. When you take the pins out, the pain has gone and it stays gone! It's not like a pill where the pain is killed for three hours and then it comes back. The thought [of acupuncture] is actually worse than going through with it.

"I first tried it with a big injury. The foot was puffy and you could see that I had damaged my toes. I had been considering acupuncture and got to the point where I was prepared to do anything because I knew that the injury was serious and I felt that anything that would get me back [to dancing] was worth it. What is interesting is that I was quite ready to believe that acupuncture wouldn't work! I had a pain at the bottom of my foot and after a couple of treatments there was no improvement and the doctor himself was a little perplexed. Then he applied the needles in different places. It killed me when the needles went in, but when he took them out it was a little better. I was so relieved when it happened, because when you're in the mood to work and something like an ache or a pain stops you it's frustrating.

"The number of treatments I take varies. One season I didn't go at all, and during a later season I went quite frequently. I had an ankle injury that acupuncture didn't actually get rid of but it helped it get well, and when I started dancing again the ankle would react to whatever I did. Some days I would overdo it, and then I would get a treatment, after which I could work on the ankle again. I did that for one entire season, and I know I would have been out again if it hadn't been for acupuncture."

In order to establish the exact nature of an injury, Dr. Hsu feels the pulse on each wrist. From the three fingers applied to each one an acupuncturist picks up twelve aspects connected with the following organs: heart, liver, spleen, lungs, kidney, stomach, large intestine, small intestine, urinary bladder, gallbladder, Sanjiao (upper, middle, and lower part of the body cavity), and finally the pericardium (the membranous sack enclosing the heart). After he has felt the pulse, said Dr. Hsu, he knows the extent of an injury. He then asks the patient for the history of the complaint, and makes his diagnosis.

Number and placement of needles varies with each ailment, as does the type of needle used. The size of a needle depends on the part of the body into which it is to be inserted, stated Dr. Hsu. "In fleshy parts, for example, the abdomen, you can apply long, large needles. On the hand you can only use small ones. No needle draws blood if it is properly applied."

The length of time a needle is left in place differs with the injury. Usually it will be from ten to thirty minutes, said Dr. Hsu, but in the case of what is known as "the buried needle" it remains in one spot for much longer. "For example, a needle can be placed in the ear, and with the application of some adhesive material, it can remain there for a whole week."

The frequency with which a patient needs treatment depends upon that person's response to it, Dr. Hsu claims. If response is good, three treatments may be sufficient. Otherwise, it may take up to ten applications, considered the usual complete course of acupuncture treatment. Dr. Hsu added that it is important not to stop before a course of treatment has taken effect. Should a patient discontinue at a time when only the symptoms are gone but not the root of the trouble, the interference serves only to prolong treatment. If a course of treatment proves ineffective, then needles must be applied in different places.

Fear of the needles can negate the effectiveness of acupuncture, Dr. Hsu stated, and in such cases he tries to alleviate reluctance by putting a needle into his own hand. Once a patient realizes there is nothing to fear, he tends to relax. Dr. Hsu maintains a person should never be forced to accept acupuncture, but in his experience, dancers are not afraid of being treated and almost without exception those who have consulted him have found the needles have helped cure their injuries.

A major injury usually is very traumatic for a dancer. Frustration, self-doubt, fear of the implications of acute pain, and of the possible reoccurrence of such a setback, can all take their toll and cause severe emotional upset. Merrill Ashley spoke for many when she said: "Frustration is what stops a lot of people [from dancing]. It stops those you don't hear about. They can't deal with the frustration or the pain, or the constant getting back into shape after taking time off. You definitely learn how to come back after injuries. It's very tricky. You have to be very patient and sensitive to what your body is trying to tell you. People tell you to come back slowly, to be careful and not to overdo it. One day your injury may not be hurting so you think it's fine and go full-out, and then the next morning it's back."

Incapacitating injuries can take many forms. In 1976, Anthony Dowell suffered a neck injury that kept him away from dance for a year. Generally speaking, Mr. Dowell has suffered comparatively few injuries because of both his professionalism and the added blessing of a perfectly proportioned body. The injury was a double blow, since he was scheduled to create Crown Prince Rudolf in *Mayerling*, choreographed by Kenneth MacMillan. "There was a point when I was seeing several people about the injury and I became very scared. There was a possibility of its being a viral infection rather than a mechanical defect. As so little is known about viruses, I got very frightened and had visions of its suddenly taking over. There was nerve damage and the muscles used to keep the shoulder blade in place weren't being used; consequently they had wasted, and that scared me. I was using other muscles to lift my arm, but you could see that one side of my back was slightly concave. Then I suddenly got scared, not only of never being able to dance again, but of having to face a physical defect. That was terrifying. Luckily, it only lasted a few days and I battled through it. Now it sounds very dramatic, but those were the thoughts that went through my mind, because as a dancer you always think physically and mechanically and this wasn't something I had entertained before. I was never in a state of panic, because I think really I did believe that I was going to come back. I thought that if I could get back I should, having got so far. I felt there was still quite a bit to achieve and, hopefully, have created for me. Having this God-given talent, which I believe in, I felt it should be used to the maximum. Once I had that straight in my head, the time off was really wonderful.

"When I first saw my neurologist, he said I really needed complete rest, and that I should stop for a month. It was just at a time when I thought I could not take time off, so rather than take his advice, I just kept going. Then, of course, after I had worked for about another six weeks, the recovery period was prolonged.

"The worst part of an injury is having colleagues give advice about who to see. You feel if you don't follow them up they think you don't want to get better. So you go through an awful period of shopping around for different opinions. Then, once the decision is made, the cloud is lifted."

Gary Chryst was interviewed while in bed with a broken leg. In the course of six weeks of lying there he experienced the gamut of emotions. "I went through a period of being in a terrible frame of mind where I was not even answering the telephone. All of a sudden you look at your life and there's no money, no pay, and to finish it, a flaw in your insurance policy! The company was off and I was taking class when I broke my foot." (The insurance policy covered only the times when the Joffrey Ballet was working.) "I get disability, but not workman's compensation. And here we are. I've let my hair grow long again—something I haven't done since 1969." When Gary Chryst injured himself, he was due to perform in place of Erik Bruhn, who also had suffered an injury. "I was doing a double saut de basque battu and landed just a quarter of an inch wrong. I was jumping very well that day, but I landed on the side bone of my foot and there was a loud crack." He simulated the noise by a sharp click with his tongue, which not only effectively resembled the sound of a breaking bone but vividly depicted the pain that accompanied it. "While I was still in the air, and coming down, I knew what was going to happen, and the sound of the crack was almost simultaneous." So fast did the incident happen, there was no time to change the placement of his foot as he landed. "After that, I just sat on the floor and moved to the side of the classroom on my bottom. But I did not pull a muscle, or tear any ligaments!"

When asked what the injury meant to him in terms of frustration, Mr. Chryst gave a piercing whistle. "Since I express myself so well, I feel, dance-wise, I didn't know what else I was going to do. I thought I was going to become a vegetable or do some nine-to-five job—one that settles for life. And I've done too much already. I knew I could never just settle. I wondered whether I would ever dance again—or if I even wanted to, considering the work it would take. Then there is the chance of its happening again." Even though he had been exposed to this prospect during all of his dancing life, Mr. Chryst said he had never given it a thought. "There's only one way to cope with injuries realistically. You live them; get depressed; cry, scream, kick, and punch the walls; then pass on without thinking of them again. Otherwise, I wouldn't make it. I'd never dance again." That would not only be sad, Mr. Chryst felt, but devastating for the ego.

Dr. William A. Liebler is the orthopedist consulted by Gary Chryst, and Mr. Chryst believes the doctor has a special understanding of dancers. "He appreciates that we have to dance. His attitude is that it's my problem to handle as I please. He said I should stay off for three months, which naturally horrified me, and when he saw my reaction he told me that if I wanted to get back in less time then it was up to me. I really respect that attitude! I haven't suffered any pain with the injury, except as the bone started to heal. Dr. Liebler took the cast off after only two weeks, to prevent atrophy.

"I'm so wiry, I'm not really going to lose that much [tone], but I've been doing a few sit-ups. I'm going to start back again next week by studying with Zena Rommett [leading New York teacher] and doing her floor exercises. When the plaster came off was when I suffered the most, because I had to control the foot myself. That was when I started to get down.

"I've been smoking too much because I'm *totally* frustrated. Normally I don't smoke that much. I need outlet. I've read seven books. I watch television and listen to music—mainly opera and Luciano Pavarotti. I'm crazy about opera, having danced in it with the New York City Opera in Beverly Sills's debut of *Manon*.

"My injury was inevitable because I was dancing too much. I had just finished a season. I was tired from traveling. I was going back and forth [from place to place] and my mind wasn't quite focused."

While a member of the Joffrey Ballet, Jimmy Dunne had an experience that proved what can be achieved through willpower. "On one occasion, I was doing an Alvin Ailey ballet and was late for my entrance because the zipper broke on my pants. I had to sew it up, and went onstage with the needle still hanging there! I ran backstage to get [across] to the other side, and as I turned the corner going round to the back wing, a girl was being carried off in a lift and her pointe shoe hit me in the side of the head. That caused me to turn, and consequently I banged the back of my head into a light boom. With that, a stagehand grabbed me and threw me out onstage because everyone was waiting for me to do my solo. I was dazed, and he pushed me on because the music was starting and I was supposed to be out there. He hadn't realized what had happened to me, because otherwise he wouldn't have done that. It gets so hectic sometimes backstage because there are so many things happening at once. The consensus was that I had stumbled. I did the whole variation and came offstage and passed out right on the floor. I had several exits during the variation and fainted more than once. The first time they brought me round and took me to the doctor, who asked me questions, looked into my eyes, and said I was all right to go back out again. That was not all—I also had to change costume in about forty seconds. The next section I had was very difficult. It was like a samba. I had a bolero shirt on and Denise Jackson was on top of a drum doing a toe-tap. One of the other men and I were her escorts. We had to shoulder-shimmy for about five minutes in the trio. It was exhausting, but I managed to get through the whole thing. Later they said I was perfectly on the music, but I had a strange look about me—as if I wasn't really there! After that section I blacked out and didn't go back for the finale. I was out with concussion for two weeks. The doctors said the delay was due to shock and that it's not unusual for athletes. Your body keeps going out of habit. That was quite a day!"

One of the greatest fears an injured dancer has is that he might be superseded during a prolonged absence. Merrill Ashley experienced this feeling. "At one stage I was really very worried that everyone would pass me by while I was off and that when I came back Mr. B. might not think I was as strong as before. He is very careful when people come back from bad injuries because he is afraid that pushing might hurt them again. This is especially true of young dancers if he hasn't decided exactly whether he wants to use them again or not. So you just sit there for a while and you could just die."

Possibly the only advantage to result from serious injury is that it gives dancers a chance to take extra classes and to work on weak points. Consequently, when they appear onstage again, technique and general performing ability sometimes have improved.

Although to some extent injury is inevitable for a dancer, only the isolated one is casual about the way he works and cares for his health. Most would concur with Greg Huffman: "You really do have to take care of your body. It's no good just kicking your legs, putting a little cologne behind your ears, and going onstage."

10

Diet and Health

ancers probably have the strangest eating habits of any segment of society, being caught uncomfortably between two necessities. As athletes they need fuel to burn, but as dancers they must keep their weight to the minimum. This latter applies especially to the women. Dr. E. J. Langner, an endocrinologist (with a special interest in nutrition) who treats dancers, said there is some evidence that the less a person eats, the less the body learns to survive on. Thus, people who chronically diet need to eat less. If they suddenly increase their food intake significantly, as with most people they gain weight. This can make them feel depressed, so they eat more and the cycle continues. Once they are on such a treadmill, losing the extra pounds can become a significant struggle. The majority of female dancers cannot eat the amount of food consumed by other athletes. In most cases, excess is not burned off through exercise, but simply adds to body weight. While this is attractive in sportsmen, dancers, who require a sleek body line in tights and leotards, become acutely self-conscious over the slightest weight gain.

Alexandra Danilova recalled the time when, shortly after leaving the Soviet Union, she learned the price of overeating. "We had been so hungry in Russia after the Revolution." (For several years after 1917 the food shortage was critical there.) "When we left the first place we went to was Germany, and they had so much wonderful food—everything, it seemed, served with whipped cream. I ate continuously, losing my slenderness, and eventually looked terrible. On one occasion, after I became a member of the Ballet Russe, Anton Dolin was dancing the Blue Bird and he had several different partners for the various performances, including myself. When I arrived at rehearsal he took one look at me and instantly told me, in such funny Russian, that he was a dancer, not a piano mover! Mr. Diaghilev agreed with him as to my being overweight, and told me that I could not dance anymore until I slimmed down. In tears, I went immediately to the drugstore to get slimming pills. Desperation made me take five pills instead of one, which was silly, but since that time I have been very careful never to get fat again. Allowing myself to do it made me so unhappy afterward, but I had been eating breakfast, lunch, tea, and a big meal after performing." Presumably it is her own experience that caused her to remark later: "*Il faut souffrir pour être belle.*" (One must suffer to be beautiful.)

David Howard advises dancers against eating too much meat. Some eat steak before going onstage, and this, he said, puts too much acid into the system. Black coffee is probably dancers' greatest staple because it contains no calories and the caffeine supplies a spurt of energy. Many drink an excess of it, and they can sometimes be so full of energy in class or in the studios, they give the impression of having been "wired for sound." Large quantities of coffee without adequate energy supplied by food will eventually cause problems.

Most dancers undereat or have erratic eating habits. They tend also to consume whatever is within reach when they get hungry, frequently giving little or no thought to its nutritional value. Mr. Howard said when he questions dancers as to their diet, "Four brownies in the morning and three nuts at night with two lettuce leaves" is the type of response he is given. However, as with other segments of society, there are also those who are very rigid about their diet, have regular eating habits, and stick to eating the appropriate foods.

Fad diets are common, and Dr. Langner spoke of a fourteen-year-old student who ate nothing but rice for two months. Her body sense was completely distorted, and at 83 pounds she believed herself to be the ideal weight. She was 5 feet 1 inch, had weighed 103 pounds and had purposely lost twenty pounds, because she thought it appropriate to be thin as a dancer. Usually even the smaller dancers do not drop below 90 pounds. Starr Danias believes she looks her best at 92 pounds and Patricia McBride is 95 pounds.

Dr. Langner believes dancers to be the most highly motivated group of people. As their entire lives are devoted to their work, they cannot live normal lives in any sense, particularly in terms of diet, she added. They have to treat food as part of the maintenance of their most important machines—their bodies. "Food has to be strictly business for them to work well. That means a regular, sometimes very boring diet, which revolves around what they can and can't eat, depending on performances and how much they [as individuals] can consume."

Psychological barriers can sometimes be the cause of weight gain. A dancer may be reaching a high point in his career and fears he will not achieve his goal. If he tends toward overweight, he can use that as an excuse for either not being accepted into a company or not being promoted. One of Dr. Langner's greatest successes, she said, was with a patient who did not have her contract renewed because she had gained weight after one year with a major ballet company. The dancer remained with the company but was reduced from a considerable repertoire to performing small parts two or three times a week. The girl lost weight slowly, partly because of her diet, and partly because she fell in love and became happier. By the beginning of the following season, Dr. Langner claimed, the dancer looked marvelous and was given a new contract. After that, she progressed according to her ability.

Muscle mass uses more calories than any other body component or function, states Dr. Langner, so to an extent it determines the caloric intake required by an individual. The big differences between people are in muscle mass. "Even though the women are mostly muscle, they weigh on average maybe a hundred to a hundred and five pounds. The men weigh approximately a hundred and sixty to a hundred and seventy pounds. Consequently, the amount of food required by the women is considerably less than that needed by the men." However, Patricia McBride confesses to having a voracious appetite, and also to being able to eat directly before a performance. "Pasta is one thing I cannot live without, and it's good to have before going onstage, rather than steak, which I find too heavy. Normally I eat a big meal after performing, but sometimes overtiredness stops me from eating anything. You react differently from season to season, eating much more substantially in the winter. I'm lucky, though, because Jean-Pierre is always dieting, and we even have separate foods in the refrigerator."

Concepts vary between people as to what they actually eat and the amount they believe they take in. The slim person who eats large meals may be slim because he or she eats only once a day. An individual who can never understand his or her weight gain may be forgetting regular meals and possible snacks in between.

Most male dancers do control their caloric intake, even though proportionately they probably eat more than most of the women. Peter Martins is 6 feet 2 inches and says his normal weight is about 182 pounds. One summer he admitted to having put on ten pounds, mainly because he loves pecan pie and beer. It is doubtful whether the weight gain would have been noticed by any member of the audience, because due to Mr. Martins's height, the extra pounds were not evident. He is one of the lucky few. Steven Caras admitted that once he reached the age of twenty-eight, his habit of eating yogurt for breakfast, going without food all day, and eating a large meal after a performance started to work against him. "The food just sits in my stomach and when I go to bed it finds its way to my sides. I wind up wearing food, which didn't happen when I was eighteen." Adam Lüders and Victor Castelli are two New York Ballet dancers who have no fear of gaining weight. Mr. Lüders, who is 6 feet 4 inches, says he has to consume vast amounts of food, including carbohydrates, to retain his normal weight. The same is also true of Fernando Bujones at American Ballet Theatre and George de la Peña.

One physiological problem that arises from girls being underweight is that many of them do not have periods. When they do, in most cases its occurrence is often very erratic. If people are starved, as body fat decreases the first thing that goes in a woman is her ability to menstruate. Usually, if dancers want to get pregnant, they change their life-style and gain weight.

Some dancers are vegetarians, and Dr. Langner supports the custom. However, she emphasizes they must be careful to take in enough protein to prevent problems from arising. "There shouldn't be negative effects if they're prepared to eat fish and eggs and drink milk. Otherwise, they have to be sure they combine the right foods to acquire protein. I think being a vegetarian is probably very good for the health." Dennis Nahat disagrees where dancers are concerned. "You've got to eat red meat, even if it's only three times a week. Any dancer who is a vegetarian lacks something in their performance. Red meat makes you mean; it gives you fangs! You need that to be a dancer. You need more drive than you can get from vegetables—something that sticks to the ribs. Without it you just don't have the necessary stamina. Half the dancers can't make it through these long seasons without problems."

Once Mr. Nahat caught hepatitis after eating shellfish, during a time when he was tired from overworking, but he was onstage again within three weeks. "I believe that two weeks is long enough to have to stay in bed. By the time we got to the third week, I told the doctor either to shoot me or make me well!"

A dancer's metabolism becomes used to strenuous exercise, and consequently after retirement there is a tendency to gain weight, even if food intake is not increased. Having become used to trim physiques, most dancers continue to take class every day, or at least do routine exercises at home. Apparently, they are in agreement with Leslie Caron's statement that she is "far too vain" to allow herself to put on weight.

Dr. Langner said the average dancer can be as much as thirty pounds underweight for his or her height. The average weight for a woman of 5 feet 6 inches is 135 pounds. Most dancers of that height weigh about 105 pounds, Dr. Langner estimates. The obsession with being thin is presumably in part the catalyst that has caused anorexia nervosa to be prevalent among dancers. "It is a tremendous catastrophe to these people when they are advised to put on weight. I think the only thing to do is try to get everyone to help you, especially their teachers. If you can get the people they admire to say they're looking too thin, sometimes that helps. Words from a doctor mean less to a dancer than those from their teacher. I don't think they trust the medical profession, and probably with some merit. Most doctors, when confronted with a girl of five feet six inches and a hundred and twenty pounds who says she wants to lose weight, would tell a dancer she's crazy. It's only when you deal with a lot of dancers [that] you come to understand they have to be thin to look good by today's standards. It's not necessarily good for them, but they have to look that way."

Dancers have been known to eat nothing for two days and then consume a whole box of cookies. "The very young are able to do this," claims Mr. Legrand, "because they're running on nervous energy. However, if they keep it up for too long, eventually they pay for it badly by destroying their internal organs. They ruin their health. I recall the case of a girl in the Harkness Ballet who was a brilliant dancer. She was chubby before joining the company, and then went absolutely anorexic. She was hospitalized many, many times, and was skin and bones, because she ate nothing but lettuce leaves and drank only black coffee. She then quit dancing and, after being cured, started teaching, and went from about eighty-five pounds to about a hundred and eighty pounds. That woman will almost certainly have serious health problems as a result."

Alcohol is a major problem for dancers. There is nothing wrong with a glass or two of wine, but the difficulty arises because it is usually drunk after 11:00 P.M., when dancers have their main meal of the day. They want to relax and live it up in the small way they can and there's a natural tendency to drink. If they do drink, wine is the best thing, simply because it's the lowest in calories and goes the furthest. Alcohol supplies empty calories—there are no vitamins, minerals, or other nutrients to speak of. If normal intake is 1200 calories a day and a person has three glasses of wine—that constitutes about 200. One sixth of the calories are empty—a great many for no nutritional value.

Dr. Langner advises dancers against eating little or nothing all day and consuming a large meal after a performance. "I try to encourage them to eat small amounts of good-quality food during the day—to eat when they get up and then again several hours into the day." Dancers consume large quantities of yogurt, but Dr. Langner thinks cottage cheese is a neglected food. "It's higher in protein, lower in carbohydrates, and in general is more filling. The problem is they want something portable, so cottage cheese and fruit or a couple of hard-boiled eggs and fruit are advisable. If somebody has a craving for sweets, they should try and satisfy it with fruits, vegetables, pasta, and bread, and stay away from concentrated sweets. Dancers should eat good food—not coffee and doughnuts. I try to get people off coffee—either completely, or at least to limit it to one or two cups a day. I think that coffee on an empty stomach is a major producer of anxiety and tension." Leslie Caron stated that Rudolf Nureyev does not drink coffee and that upon being told by him that it robs the body of the B vitamins she stopped drinking it herself. "Tea doesn't seem to bother people as much as coffee," continued Dr. Langner, "so I tend to tell people to drink weak tea. I also like to discuss their dinner with them, so they plan ahead, and when they go out don't go wild and order everything on the menu."

To break the habit of eating a large meal after a performance is difficult and is something most dancers are unable to achieve. Alexander Godunov says he has mainly fruit during the day and likes steak at night. "Usually I eat after a performance because when you are rehearsing and break for maybe one hour, you cannot eat much, otherwise you need rest before you can jump again." Merle Park generally eats a cooked breakfast and says she usually goes without lunch. "I'm so hungry at night, and go home and find dinner waiting for me and then go out like a light afterward. I wake up a couple of hours later and there's no tele in England because it's closed down at that time. I'm generally bad about looking after myself, and always eat a lot of cakes and buns before a big performance because I think one needs the carbohydrate. I don't drink coffee or spirits, only wine."

Dr. Hsu said that dancers should follow a general program of health with plenty of rest and sleep, and they should not overdo the exercise, or stop suddenly after strenuous activity. He added that they should not eat or drink immediately after a performance or a taxing course of exercise, but wait five or ten minutes before doing so. "It might sound ridiculous when I say that, but many dancers go right offstage and eat honey or drink ice-cold water. That is a no-no! Another point to keep in mind is that, after dancing, all the pores are open, so they should try to avoid drafts." Added Merrill Ashley, "When I finish, the first thing I do is remove my makeup, then slowly take my headpiece off and let down my hair. I don't do slow exercises after I've been dancing, but neither do I come offstage and leap into the shower."

In their student days, many dancers live on a minimal income that sometimes keeps them barely at subsistence level. Bart Cook has vivid memories of his early days in New York. "I shared an apartment with five other kids and there was never any food. We would eat spaghetti with butter on it for dinner. I don't know how I danced on that diet, except that I was so young. Now I pay attention to what I eat. My intake is less now, of necessity, but basically I eat good foods with some protein every night. I like to dance on an empty stomach when possible, but if I have to do a ballet that needs a lot of energy, I take something around three or four so that it will have time to get into my system. If I'm feeling energetic, I won't eat anything. Sometimes I have been known to consume a whole cake or box of cookies. It's like the seventh deadly sin!"

Dancers cannot afford to burn the candle at both ends. "When you're into a heavy rehearsal and performance schedule," said Patrick Bissell, "if you combine it with an active social life you get run-down and find yourself not eating. It's hard enough to make yourself eat three good meals a day. I try to do it but a lot of the time don't succeed, and go home starved. Then I'm too tired to fix myself anything. I'm often too exhausted even to go to a restaurant, and end up grabbing a sandwich, and find myself getting run-down."

Twenty-twenty vision is important to dancers. Without it it is difficult to assess spacing between them, and sometimes they cannot see clearly enough to relate to anything. Merrill Ashley wears contact lenses. "I can dance without them, but don't like to, and it takes me a week or so to adjust. There was an occasion when I couldn't wear them for a couple of weeks because I had an eye infection, and the first few days my balance was completely gone. Your whole perspective changes. That happens to a great many people in the company. If you can't wear contact lenses it's difficult, but you get used to it."

Most dancers who smoke do so to excess, which is paradoxical considering the energy they expend to constantly improve their bodies. Lung capacity is of prime importance for a dancer, but many have convinced themselves that because of their general physical fitness, nicotine passes through their systems fast enough to have minimal negative effect. "I don't think all the hard breathing cleans out their systems," verified Dr. Hamilton. "The smokers are short-winded compared to the other dancers." He believes dancers smoke for a variety of reasons, and mentioned nervousness, insecurity, the long hours of work, and a desire to stay thin as possibilities. Said Greg Huffman, "Being physical is a very important part of being healthy, and I'm sure if I didn't smoke I would have almost too much energy! I'd be so healthy, it would be unbearable! There is such discipline in our lives, and I think man is basically self-destructive anyway. It's just part of human nature."

Performers are subjected to abnormal amounts of stress, and those dancers who are vulnerable to it will take it more seriously than they would if they were in less taxing occupations, said psychologist Dr. Albert Ellis. Most people are in a position to take time away from work if they are not feeling well, but usually a dancer wants to appear onstage to avoid disappointing an audience, or himself. If a performance is scheduled, he will appear under most circumstances, preparing himself with bandages or aspirin and dancing in pain, or with a high temperature, if necessary.

Narcissism is a weakness to which nearly all humans are prey, believes Dr. Ellis. He thinks maybe it is associated with dancers more than with many other people, only because of the hours dancers spend concentrating on their bodies and working in front of mirrors, which can give the impression of their being narcissistic. Yet their bodies must be in excellent condition, and their line refined if they are to perform. Far from being egocentric, the majority of them are relentlessly self-critical.

"Practically no dancer is masochistic," continued Dr. Ellis. "When they go for pain, they're really trying to go for some of the pleasure—a hair shirt is a way to try and get into heaven! Dancers' basic goal is not masochistic. They take present pain for future gain, and have more discipline than most people, who would not become dancers because it requires too much hard work. Most of the population goes for present pleasure for future pain by smoking, drinking, overeating, etc. In some respects, this makes outstanding dancers saner than other people. Now if the future gain is only ego—killing yourself in order to get famous—then that's another matter. The goal in life is to enjoy, not be approved by others. However, some have a dire necessity to be approved, and all artists, especially performers, have that need more than most people."

11

Looking Ahead

*F*acing retirement is possibly life's most difficult hurdle for the majority of people. It is not necessarily the type of work that will be missed, but the fact of being useful, feeling needed, that one was making a worthwhile contribution to society. When the day comes for dancers to retire, they can suffer withdrawal pains for two years or more. For those known internationally, leaving the stage can be especially difficult. Unlike people who perform a service or manufacture a product, dancers are their own product. Every time they appear they are tested anew, for each is only as good as his last performance. For those who feel the fantasy of the stage acutely, or who believe the only area of life in which they can excel is dance, it is devastating to have the emotional outlet removed. Added to that are the very definite highs or momentary thrills that are present when the body combines with all its sensibilities in performing a pirouette or double cabriole. Rebecca Wright maintains that for a minute particle of time the former places a dancer on another plane. "A single pirouette lasts for maybe one second, yet within it a moment of infinity exists when you don't know where you are."

Dancers confess to being unable to recognize when they are at their peak, yet all too easily can tell when their technique is slipping. Faced with that harsh reality, for a time most take advantage of their developing artistry and are appreciated as mature artists. Audiences, as well as dancers, love the security of familiarity. The day favorite performers leave the stage after long careers, they leave their followers with only an image traced in their minds, and perhaps films to help keep that image alive. Occasionally a dancer is born who fuses technique and artistry with such force that like a tiny sun he pours forth his warm rays on the people who come to see him, charging them with his powerful charisma. Such a dancer is hard to say good-bye to.

Timing of retirement is all-important as to the memories dancers leave behind. Some are unable to accept the passsage of time and hang on, terrified by the prospect of any other way of life.

Few careers can be as tenuous as that of a ballet dancer. Those whose ambition is to make their mark on ballet history must be prepared to take tremendous risks onstage as they work to develop their technique and artistry. The search for perfection never ceases. Pushing just beyond the limit each time they perform exposes them to an exceptionally high risk of injury. They must live on the edge to succeed. Like others in high-risk activities, such as motor racing, of necessity they "draw the curtain" against what for them could be fatal injury; otherwise they could never continue to challenge fate with such bravado. Though it might seem unrealistic for dancers not to have an alternative occupation to fall back on, for some it is part of the inability to accept the possibility of enforced early retirement. Some progress naturally into other aspects of the dance. Natalia Makarova said she wants to continue dancing while she feels she is improving, yet she stages ballets, choreographs, coaches, and for one season had her own company. Merle Park, who believes a dancer reaches maturity somewhere between thirty-five and fifty, will continue to dance as long as possible, for the same reason as Miss Makarova. However, already she has opened a ballet school in London, because she loves to teach.

Peter Martins is regarded by many as the natural and obvious successor to George Balanchine at the New York City Ballet. "It's really hard for me to say whether I would like to take over City Ballet because it is like tying a noose around your own neck," maintained Mr. Martins. "Nobody will succeed on the level that Balanchine has, and everybody has to realize that. On the other hand, I say that Balanchine will outlast my dancing career. He can direct that company from anywhere. If he wants to sit in his country house he can do it over the phone. The company is so strongly structured that it's not going to change if he's not around for two weeks. When the time comes for somebody else to take over, I don't think it is going to be a point of who wants to—it's more a question of who feels the most responsibility. Already I have an enormous commitment to the company, although I don't know how long that will last. Maybe somebody else will come up who will feel more responsible. It's very much of a family as a company and the dancers have to like the director, otherwise they don't enjoy dancing."

Mr. Martins spoke of his own future. "I can't anticipate how long I will be onstage. I look at some people who are still performing in their forties, and it's a struggle. I don't know if I would like to see myself like that. Also, I function very well when I'm not onstage. I don't live for it—unlike many great dancers who really die when they're not performing. Maybe that's good, but maybe it's the one thing that's lacking in my dance—that absolute vampire element, as with the way Rudi sticks his teeth in. I can't change, though, as it wouldn't be natural. Erik Bruhn and Margot have that vampire element too, I think, and I don't know who else is great, apart from Mischa, who I don't see at all like that. I identify with Mischa. We are a little bit alike that way. Whatever comes naturally we do." In September 1980, while still dancing, Mikhail Baryshnikov became director of American Ballet Theatre. At the New York City Ballet Peter Martins was appointed a ballet master in the fall of 1981.

There are certain methods that can be used to help prolong a dance career. David Howard said that a dancer must understand the body, work it correctly, align it properly, avoid forcing the joints and overstretching them, and pay attention to routine health care. Modern teaching methods pay much more attention to the training the body needs to be able to perform to current standards without forcing, maintains Mr. Howard. At one time a dancer was told what to do without any regard for the stresses and strains on the body. Nowadays, he added, despite the greater demands in performance, the average length of a dancer's career has been prolonged. Mr. Howard cited Alicia Alonso as a dancer with a highly developed understanding of her body. Despite being blind, and over sixty, Miss Alonso still dances leading roles with the Ballet Nacional de Cuba, the company she helped create after the Cuban Revolution in 1959.

Body type is a contributing factor with regard to longevity. One reason Dame Margot Fonteyn was able to dance until sixty was because she was perfectly proportioned. The looser the joints and tendons and the longer the muscles, the better the chance of a prolonged career. Scott Barnard eleborated: "Doing three ballets a night in a company is not abusing the body, because that maintains stamina. Not taking classes abuses the body. It must be kept supple. Those dancers who don't do that are shortening their careers every day."

Andrei Kramarevsky, who teaches at the School of American Ballet and is a former principal of the Bolshoi Ballet, emphasized that from the age of thirty-eight a dancer should not perform more than three times a week. Rudolf Nureyev still appears onstage about two hundred times a year, which Mr. Kramarevsky claims is bad for the muscles.

Twenty-eight is the age at which muscles begin to lose their suppleness, in Bart Cook's experience. Since then, he said, he has had to do considerably more work to keep his body stretched out.

Anthony Dowell said that, ideally, he schedules three full-length ballets a week, with adequate time away from the stage in between. He appears on three consecutive days only in one-act ballets, such as *Shadowplay* and *Contredances* with American Ballet Theatre, and *A Month in the Country, Hamlet, Rhapsody, Symphonic Variations,* and *Daphnis and Chloë* with the Royal Ballet.

The majority of men and women retire from the stage by the time they are forty; of those who continue after that, few are men. This is mainly attributable to the heavy demands of partnering and bravura technique.

Robert Weiss, who has always had to contend with a tight body, injured his Achilles tendon in 1980 and returned to the stage in 1981. Prior to that, when discussing retirement he said, "It's very difficult to adjust to something else when you've spent your whole life as a dancer. Power corrupts in one sense, wealth in another, and certainly adulation and stardom corrupt in their ways."

Ivan Nagy, determined to leave the stage before his dancing declined, disappointed numerous balletgoers when he retired at thirty-five. Watching the success of some nineteen- and twenty-year-olds in American Ballet Theatre, and aware of how young "old age" sets in among dancers, he declared before his final performance, "Today I feel like a wax-museum piece. Tomorrow [in the outside world] I shall be young again!"

Many great dancers continue to devote their lives to ballet after leaving the stage. Dame Alicia Markova coaches and lectures. Dame Margot Fonteyn coaches, makes educational films, writes books, lectures, and appears in certain roles, such as that of Lady Capulet in *Romeo and Juliet* with La Scala Opera Ballet at the Metropolitan Opera House in 1981. As teaching and coaching are her fortes, Alexandra Danilova now passes on her expertise to students at the School of American Ballet. Erik Bruhn travels internationally, coaching dancers in the world's leading companies, and Ivan Nagy is the artistic director of the ballet company at the Teatro Municipal in Santiago, Chile, occasionally traveling to coach.

As each outstanding dancer passes on his or her expertise to talented fledglings, the vital link ensures that classical ballet will continue to flourish. In 1980, sixteen-year-old Nancy Raffa came to the attention of Natalia Makarova, and she has become the renowned ballerina's protégée and is sometimes partnered by Fernando Bujones. In the fall of 1981 Miss Raffa was given a contract by American Ballet Theatre. Meanwhile, at the New York City Ballet, Darci Kistler, also sixteen, had principal roles choreographed on her by Jerome Robbins and Peter Martins, and was promoted to soloist in the fall of 1981.

The tradition continues as each artist, a small part of the essence of God, serves to make man's life that much the richer.

Index

Page numbers in italics refer to illustrations.